HEROES AND ROSES

HEROES AND ROSES

Arnold L. Haskell

A View of Bulgaria

DARTON, LONGMAN & TODD · LONDON

DARTON LONGMAN & TODD LTD
64 Chiswick High Road London W4

© 1966 Arnold L. Haskell

First published 1966

Printed in Great Britain by Cox and Wyman Limited
London, Fakenham and Reading

For Donka with love and through her
to the magnificent young people of Bulgaria,
the nation's greatest wealth

CONTENTS

LIST OF PLATES

A NOTE ON THE ARTIST
PENCHO KOULEKOV

Pencho Koulekov was born in 1924 of a poor peasant family in the village of Hirevo, Gabrovo. He served in the army, fighting against the Germans in 1944–5. In 1955 he graduated from the Nikolai Pavlovich Academy of Art, specialising in graphic art. He has exhibited in Sweden, Denmark, Italy, Austria, the USSR, China and elsewhere and has had an immensely successful one man show in Sofia.

He is noted for his landscapes, architectural drawings and his studies of peasant life and especially for his interpretation of historical scenes inspired by old chronicles and manuscripts.

I am greatly indebted to the artist and the Foreign Languages Press for the use of works that convey so admirably the traditions of the country.

ACKNOWLEDGEMENTS

I am greatly indebted to the following for their hospitality, help and understanding. Dr Peter Voutov, Minister of Culture during my visits and Mr Angel Boudev, Deputy Minister. Mr P. Bozov, Cultural attaché in London who has been consistently helpful. To, the Foreign Relations Committee, Mr Andreev and Mr Alexander Belkovsky, chief of protocol and a mine of historical information. To the Concert Direction, my special friends; Mr Yordan Kindalov, its director during my first visit, and his wife, Mr Angelov, Mr Dobri Dobrev, Mr Dimitrov, Mr Kainarov and Mrs Miloshova. To Mr Bratanov, of the Revolutionary Museum, for much research on my behalf, to Mrs Alexieva, for a stimulating conversation and for the many quotations from her admirable translations and from the works in English published by her organisation. To Mr Velichko Peychev of Balkantourist for information and photographs. To that superb artist Katya Popova and her husband Dr Radomir Vassilev, for their warm friendship.

To Miss Liliana Vesselinova and Miss Marta Mihailova and especially to my dear friends and companions, Milen Paunov and Donka Minkova, who were tireless on my behalf. To Mrs Paunov and to Mr D. Paunov, who painted for me a picture that I greatly value. Nor would I like my gratitude to my wife to be taken for granted; her Russian and her criticism have proved invaluable.

To the Directors of the National Opera and Theatre. To the drivers Eftim Georgiev and my old friend Stoyan, who showed me so much of their country. To Madame Batinove, who showed me Liliana Dimitrova's house in Plovdiv, and to the many others I met daily, colleagues in the ballet, journalists, hoteliers and passers-by.

The material was theirs, the opinions mine alone. They may disagree with some of them; they cannot doubt my deep love for their country.

In 1860 Lord Strangford discovered 'a Bulgarian people with a past history and a possible future'. *'Among all the Balkan nations it is the Bulgarians who have the sterling qualities which appeal to English sympathies.'*

'The Bulgarians would be the most prosperous and contented population in the world under a government that had their prosperity at heart.'

G. Muir Mackenzie and A. P. Irby 1867

1. INTRODUCTORY

A DECLARATION OF POLITICAL BAGGAGE

The early traveller to eastern Europe had the considerable advantage of tales of hardship and sometimes of narrow escapes to enliven his narrative. He was writing of the unknown and so bringing vicarious adventure and also a feeling of cradled cosiness to the library subscriber in the cathedral close. Only a hundred years ago two remarkable women, the Misses Muir Mackenzie and Irby, rode four times across the Turkish occupied provinces in Europe to write a shrewd, vivid and prophetic account of the Balkans. Today tourists in their thousands are flown over to those same places as part of a package deal and when they arrive they find on the surface very much the same things that they left behind them. What a world of difference between the words 'traveller' and 'tourist'. Today even the tourist is outnumbered by the holidaymaker and the main reason for travel is the quest for the sun. It is reassuring to many while basking to find such home comforts as a well-brewed cup of tea. I do not decry such physical holidays, but what is really stimulating is to note the differences in outlook and customs, to get to know a people and to realise that in so doing there are other types of adventure still possible.

This then is not a guide book but a series of very personal impressions of a country in which I worked and where in the course of my work I met very many people in a thoroughly relaxed manner. My main concern was not so much with places and

monuments as with the people who live there and built them. I
have of course described and commented on the places which
interested me and helped to build up my picture. It is most certainly not a political treatise, but no book about a people and their
way of life can ignore politics and still attempt a worthwhile picture. To deal with a glorious history and an advanced culture in
terms of waitresses, hotel porters and taxi drivers would be an
insult.

I have found, from long experience of work and travel in communist countries, that even should I wish to ignore politics
altogether I am, on my return home, willy-nilly forced into what
often becomes a heated political discussion, generally with people
who have never visited the countries concerned, studied Marx-
Lenin or seen communism at work. My likes and dislikes in opera,
ballet, food and wine are accepted or discounted through an
irrelevant prejudice. They say you are brainwashed; that is when
they concede that you have a brain at all. There has been too much
'no plug in the bath' type of criticism, too many of those mythical
ego-boosting tales of having been shadowed or spied upon. The
only time I have been shadowed, and it does inflate one's ego, was
in Sardinia during my honeymoon. The agent was a delightful
man and told me that as the government was not paying him very
much for his services he would be pleased, for a small fee, to act as
our guide. The arrangement was highly satisfactory; he proved
an excellent guide.

It is essential for me therefore before crossing the frontier to
declare, as far as I can, my political baggage.

I am so strongly politically interested that I am committed to no
party. Perhaps, as that famous 'floating voter' wooed by all parties,
I am something of an anarchist. Of late, especially in international
relations, the current has borne me very much to the left of centre.
I have come more and more to respect communism as an ideal and
a valid way of life. I believe it to be well suited to the actual conditions and the historical background of some countries but not of
others and to have many achievements, material and spiritual, to
its credit, not only where it is established but as a pace-setter
throughout the world. The history of east-west relations since 1917

shows that the east has more often than not 'been on the side of the angels', even though it would express it differently.

I deplore the facile slogans 'iron curtain' and 'free world', just as I deplore the label 'fascist', accompanied by the usual unimaginative epithets, for anyone who is not a committed Marxist. There is a curtain of fog that, given goodwill and common sense on both sides, is penetrable. Semantics should be taught in all schools. Freedom or democracy, whatever meaning one gives them, are not the monopoly of any one party. There are, moreover, various applications of communism just as there are various applications of Christianity; these vary according to history, geography and national temperament. The communist world is coming to realise this. Stalinism was an aberration as much to be deplored as the Inquisition. It took place in a country that had produced Ivan the Terrible and a long line of not unworthy successors.

I write as a Catholic. The founder of Christianity may or may not have been a communist *avant l'heure*. The point has been hotly debated by many churchmen; it seems to me irrelevant. One thing is absolutely certain: he was no upholder of capitalism and stated with unmistakable vehemence that the rich man's chances of reaching heaven were negligible. There is nothing in his teaching to outlaw economic communism and I sympathise with the many logical Latins in France and Italy who feel drawn to both camps. A Catholic-communist dialogue in the spirit of Pope John is both possible and desirable.* Palmiro Togliatti from the communist side called for the same thing in his testamentary memorandum, and the Russians today deplore puerile atheism, arguing that in the past religion has not been incompatible with progress and socialism, citing Copernicus, Campanella, Thomas More and Leo Tolstoy. It is the founder of communism who denied the possibility of any belief in the supernatural, which seems to me a weakness, confusing a particular Church at a given moment of history with the religion it professed. But was Marx not reacting against such prevalent views as Sir Randolph Churchill's who

---

* 'Since *Pacem in Terris* it may be that the social aims of Communism and Christianity are no longer seen as invariably incompatible.' *The Times*, leading article on Worker-Priests.

could write that he contemplated with alarm what would happen without religion to 'those masses of the people, who, with some hope of a happier state thereafter, were toiling their weary way through the world, content to tolerate, for a time, their less fortunate lot'? Such an attitude is impossible today. Churchman and communist have in common a desire for peace and the general good of the majority. The hymn, so consoling to the Victorian rich,

> The rich man at his castle
> The poor man at his gate
> God made them high and lowly
> He ordered their estate

is as bad Christianity as it is poor verse.

There is much room for discussion and some very solid grounds for agreement. Theology apart, the doctrine of original sin is superb psychology and sound common sense for Catholic and communist alike. Fascism is original sin carried to its extreme limit, the end product of egoism. It is not an ideology but a positive evil. It cannot be equated with communism, as is sometimes glibly done, in spite of communism's one-party system and its sombre record of Stalinist terror. It was not invented by Mussolini or improved upon by Hitler. It existed before them and it exists after them. It has many disguises; it can on occasion speak through the voice of cardinal, commissar or of the professional patriot elected to his country's legislature by due democratic process. It invented the homicidal slogan, 'better dead than red' to throw dust in the eyes of the feeble-minded, it has brought misery through dubious and bloodthirsty adventures in Latin America and Vietnam. Surely here is common ground enough, with each side sticking to its ideals, for something less negative than coexistence.

This is more than a 'declaration of political baggage', it is directly involved with my subject, Bulgaria, for it is in this atmosphere, as we shall see, brought about by the experience of an exceptional history, that a small country can harbour a great influence.

I am most certainly neither naïve nor callous enough to believe that the alternative to communism is capitalism backed up by napalm and the marines. This is as out of date as the missionary, gunboat and trader sequence. It gives one a shock to realise that in what passes as the richest country in the world there is so much abject poverty side by side with so much ostentatious wealth, the 'two worlds' surviving into the mid twentieth century. No wonder that with such a way of life the communist party is banned. The rich man on the barricades is a singularly unpleasant sight.

I have discussed politics freely in Bulgaria and other communist countries, both with party members and others. Of course, I met many who had criticisms to make, some who were disgruntled and whose ideals had suffered a shock, but never did I meet anyone who wished to be 'liberated', to return to the old days or who looked to the west for a way of life, much though they may have liked its consumer goods, its pop songs or its abstract art. The young in particular were enthusiastic about the advances that had been made and the opportunities given them. At times they may have found Pater a little too strict but their patriotism was never in doubt.

It is a mistake, an easy one to make, to imagine because of the conformism of certain externals that all communist countries are identical. There are the banners and those modern ikons, the blown up photographs of political leaders, the youth parades and gymnastic festivals, the peace slogans on bridges and railway stations and the roadside portraits of shock workers, the massive granite statues and the neon-lighted five-pointed stars on the summit of ornate buildings, the party cathedrals. There is the welcome absence of commercial advertising with its blatant sex symbols and the lack of variety in the comparatively few cars; the big *Chaika*, chauffeur-driven cars, inevitably belong to ministers.

These externals bear witness to and may in their turn produce a certain uniformity of outlook and conduct, but far less than one would think. Bulgaria differs as greatly from the Soviet Union as Switzerland from Great Britain, and Great Britain from the United States.

As Russia, a country that I love and respect, is the parent of communism and the most written about, often inaccurately, it is useful to establish some differences. The communist belief is the

B

same and Bulgaria is the most attuned to Moscow for reasons that
we shall see. Russia has throughout her history been more secretive
and suspicious of foreigners. Her civil war was long and painful
and from the first she suffered from a foolish and unjust interven-
tion. This has left its mark. The Russian is more mystically inclined than the down to earth Bulgarian and this is reflected in his
politics. In Russia the tourist trade, important though it is, is an
incidental, in Bulgaria it has become an increasingly vital part of
the economy. In all eastern European countries the people are
interested in and welcome foreigners. In Bulgaria they are freer to
do so, since the visitors come there for a carefree holiday and are
largely unconscious of the fact that they are in a communist
country at all. No one can visit the Soviet Union without some
reaction to communism; it tends to be regarded as all black or all
white. The role of the intelligentsia in Russia is ambivalent. They
were the spearhead of the revolution and at the same time they are
often suspect as liberals. Bulgaria has an inbuilt democracy, with
peasant, worker and intellectual in a closer-knit society.

Wherever I travel I hope that I am a fellow-traveller and a
comrade in the finest sense of those admirable, highly religious and
much abused words.

This book then deals with the way that I set out to know the
Bulgarians. I make no apology for much use of the personal pro-
noun; it is far less egotistic and dogmatic than an attempt to write
a textbook about Bulgaria, its people and its economy, for which in
any case I am not qualified. It is, as I have written, a by-product
of work done there, as was *Waltzing Matilda*, my previous book of
travel in Australia. As in that book it will tell of the particular
quality of excitement that my quest to discover a people gave me.
It is in some sort the story of a love affair between a man and a
country that has made the words 'Bulgaria' and 'the Balkans' of
very special significance to me. This does not mean that there can
be no criticism, none of the light and shade of a hot summer's day
on Vitosha mountain. I shall most certainly be accused of wearing
a pair of rose-coloured spectacles. I can only say that I write of
what I saw and felt. Had I not been attracted in the first place I
would never have written this book.

I hope that the reader's reaction will be that this is a country to visit, to discover and to linger in, that it holds something more than sandy beaches, comfortable hotels and smiling faces, though these exist in plenty.

BULGARIA OUT OF THE BLUE

My introduction to Bulgaria was sudden and totally unexpected. My ignorance was complete. I had no facts nor fancies, not even sufficient for an erroneous picture. On a psychiatrist's couch my only association with the country would have been the words, 'Gladstone and Bulgarian atrocities', 'yoghourt', which last I soon discovered was not known under that name any more than caviare is caviare to the Russians. The only Bulgarians I knew by repute were a mixed bag: 'Foxy' Ferdinand, the King of World War I, Dimitrov, the first man to stand up to and so reveal the weakness of the Nazis, and the distinguished singers, Boris Christoff and Nikolai Giaurov. I also knew that Mr Bloom was offering tours of Bulgaria to the housewives who purchased his washing-machines. This last a distinctly off-putting piece of information.

One Monday morning, on coming to my study at the Royal Ballet School, my secretary told me that Mr Bozov, the Bulgarian cultural attaché, was coming to see me in an hour's time. Such visits were not infrequent and they usually heralded a group of balletomanes or journalists armed with cameras and notebooks. The school always aroused more interest abroad than it did in England. I had my words of welcome and my little speech prepared. Punctually to the minute, Mr Bozov was shown in. It was he who made the speech. He was inviting me to Varna as the guest of the Bulgarian Concert Direction to act as one of the judges of the first international dance contest for soloists under thirty years of age. I accepted even before he had finished talking. It was a few months before my retirement and I needed just such a change. Galina Ulanova was to preside and there was no one in the world of ballet I loved or respected more. It seemed a wonderful opportunity for a lesson in an art that I had spent a lifetime in studying. Eastern Europe appealed to me, especially the sunshine of my favourite Black Sea with its nostalgic memories of Yalta and Gurzouf. My only condition was that I travel by land.

THE CONTEST IN ITS CONTEXT

My journey was a leisurely one giving me a twelve hour break in Munich. What a beautiful, prosperous and cultured city with its cheerful, well fed, industrious and essentially 'cosy' people in *lederhosen* and *dirndl*, goggling at the many shop windows draped with every variety of delicatessen, or sitting in cellars and *Konditorei* drinking beer or *café mit schlag* while consuming mounds of pastry. Everyone I spoke to, and how welcoming they were, seemed to have a vivid and convenient memory, one that worked from 1946 onwards. They talked of their friendship with their great American allies and of the work they had done for them. Coca Cola had penetrated in a big way into this stronghold of beer. When they heard I was English they told me how much they liked the English, and after all we had so much in common. They spoke, almost possessively, of their great admiration for *V*inston Churchill. Nearly everyone spoke the language with transatlantic fluency. However, the signposts to Dachau and the surviving massive architecture of the Third Reich made me wonder whether this 'cosiness' was not the supreme secret weapon of the Germans, all the more dangerous because they themselves were not aware of it. A divided Germany seemed to me a very good thing, especially when I remembered a visit to the occupied Rhineland in 1919 with very similar reactions from the Germans, only I believed them then and, God forgive me, thought that the realistic French lacked understanding.

I arrived in Sofia late at night, hoping that nothing had gone wrong with the arrangements and that I would be met. I was, by the flashes of a battery of press photographers who fixed my unshaven and travel-stained face, a bunch of cellophane-robed flowers, always embarrassing to an Englishman, and some very hearty handshakes. I was then bundled into a car with one of my greeters. To my relief he spoke fluent English. He introduced himself as Milen Paunov, tenor at the Sofia opera. He was to be my constant companion from that moment and to become a valued friend. The next day we wandered round Sofia and after a couple of good meals and two acts of *Rigoletto* I was put into the sleeper for Varna. Paunov was to follow. His parting advice to me was, 'if in any difficulty, speak Russian'. As my Russian is scanty and Russian and Bulgarian are two very different languages this was far from reassuring.

A train journey in eastern Europe is always rewarding, the traveller is an object of interest and a subject for hospitality. I shared my supper and spoke to guard and passengers in a mixture of languages. I no longer felt on my own. On arrival at Varna I was greeted by still more photographers, a posse of reporters – 'how do you like Bulgaria? What do you think of the contest?' – the customary bunches of flowers and an even larger welcoming committee, headed by Yordan Kindalov, director of the Concert Direction and my host.

The contest more than lived up to my expectations, I will write of this and the other contests at length in the appropriate place. It had started as the whole object of my visit but it was soon to find its place in the context of Bulgaria. It was the genial Kindalov who suggested that in my spare time I see as much as possible of Bulgaria and who lent me his car so that I could make long trips (off the well-trodden tourist track) with Paunov and the admirable driver Stoyan.

I welcomed this, especially as there had already been many opportunities to meet Bulgarians and I had been greatly impressed. This came about through the translation arrangements made for the contest. The judges between them spoke sixteen different languages and the Concert Direction had provided a remarkable corps of linguists. They were mostly university students in their final year, fluent in their chosen language, cheerful, independent minded, discussing every subject under the sun with enormous animation and humour. I have seen suspicion and fear; there were neither here. No one said: 'on no account write this', or 'whatever you do don't mention my name'. And they knew I was a writer. They spent most of the time with us, both on and off duty, and it was through them that we met young Bulgaria. One particular girl, Violetta, a twenty year old, who translated for my Cuban friends

Alicia and Fernando Alonso, spoke Spanish, English, French, Russian and Czech with ease. As a parting gift for Alicia she had sat up all night to copy the music of a dance by a Russian composer that she had borrowed for the purpose from an East German competitor. From the very first, therefore, this became much more than a dance contest, however interesting that was in itself. Certainly these translators were handpicked for their skill and intelligence, but not for any other reason. Some came from families who were party members, the new aristocracy, the majority not; one was a churchgoer and told me so. All of them were patriots, proud of their history and traditions though they never rammed information, statistical or otherwise, down our throats. They had, as I was to find in nearly all Bulgarians, the blessed gift of laughter. I made many friends that year with whom I have corresponded and whom I have met again.

At the final banquet – banquets were held on every possible occasion – after a ballet gala at the Sofia Opera House where the prime minister, Todor Zhivkov and members of the government entertained us, I found myself highly elated by that evening's performance with Maximova and Vassiliev at their dazzling best, by all that I had experienced and, no doubt at all, by copious draughts of wine. I proposed a toast. This was the custom at every meal, let alone at banquets in spite of an admirable national proverb that 'those who are thirsty do not drink toasts'. I raised my glass 'to the country's greatest wealth, the young people of Bulgaria'. My toast became a speech. I commented with some vehemence on the negative aspects of soapsud publicity, stressed the grand scale of the cultural activities and generally let myself go. I wound up by saying that I would like to visit the country for a longer period and to write a book about it, dedicated to those many young friends whose toast I was proposing. I felt I had been a little rash but before I had time to become self-conscious, Dr Peter Voutov, the Minister of Culture, who speaks English fluently and whom I had already met many times, said that he would take me at my word and that, if I wished to return, he would give me every facility. 'Consider yourself free to go anywhere, meet anyone and write anything. Remember not to overlook our failings.' He went on to

say that he hoped that I would talk to as many people as possible –
'just stop them in the street and talk' – and not merely visit monuments, though I would find the monuments a valuable background.
He would give me neither briefing nor guidance but I could call on
him and his colleagues at all times for any help that I might need.
We filled our glasses and drank another half-dozen toasts or so.

On the very day that I returned to England the washing-machine
empire collapsed into bubbles and scum; part of my speech at any
rate had been justified.

And so a year later I returned for a prolonged stay, having in the
meantime done my homework with some care.

PART ONE
People and Places

2. BACKGROUND TO BULGARIA

HOMEWORK

Before setting out I asked a friend who had written a delightful and immensely successful travel book what method he had adopted. 'The recipe is simple,' he told me. 'Visit the country and have a thoroughly good time, then come home and paraphrase the article in the *Encyclopaedia Britannica*.' It is certain that my friend did not follow his own advice. It is equally certain that many of my readers will be as ignorant of Bulgaria as I was, so that I make no apology by beginning with the briefest digest of my homework. I can promise that it will be almost the only occasion that I shall refer to statistics and bare facts. I must, I suppose, also run the risk of it being the only occasion upon which I shall be completely accurate. Facts, however, are selective and I do not claim objectivity; my reason for writing the book was my intense attraction to the country and its people. In any case I mistrust professions of 'objectivity' and the reader has been warned.

Bulgaria is a country of about eight million inhabitants, less than that of Greater London. Of these 88 per cent are Bulgarians, 8·6 Turks, 2·6 gypsies and there are a small number of Armenians, Russians, Greeks and Jews. There is no minority problem and the racial and cultural homogeneity is obvious from border to border. It has an area of 42,818 square miles, smaller than that of England with 50,871 square miles. The smallness of the country makes its achievements all the more impressive. 'Nothing is impossible to a Bulgarian,' is a popular saying, However, this requires an effort since it is capped by another homely proverb, 'God gives, but doesn't put it in the cowshed.'

It is roughly rectangular in shape, bounded to the north by Rumania, mainly following the line of the Danube and joined to it by the great bridge of friendship at Roussé. To the east the Black Sea separates it from the Soviet Union, to the south-east it marches with Turkey, to the south with Greece and to the south-west and the west with Yugoslavia.

For so small a country it has immense scenic variety; plains, mountains, forests, valleys and riviera and an exceptionally rich flora. The Balkan range (*Stara Planina* or old mountains), stretching from west to east divides the country into two regions. This forms a natural climatic barrier, sheltering south Bulgaria from the cold air of the north.

Is this last paragraph of any value? I doubt it. An atlas is so easily available. It hides the potent magic that the words *Stara Planina* hold for every Bulgarian, words of deep sentiment and not the facile sentimentality of popular songs about the green mountains that go down to the sea. This high range with its bosky vegetation has been the *maquis* of Bulgaria from the time of the Ottoman oppression to 1944; 'the mountain sings a *haidouk* song'. It was here that the brave *haidouti*, the men of the resistance, harassed the Turks, it was at the Shipka Pass that the Turk was finally hurled back, it was here that the partisans ambushed the Germans and their collaborators. An old folk-song tells us, 'Bulgarians are men who love the golden wheat in summer and a bowl of red wine in winter, but, if anyone wants to know what a Bulgarian is like when an enemy attacks him, let him ask the *Stara Planina'*.

The Sredna Gora mountains rise to the south of the Balkans and run parallel to them. Enclosed in the middle is the most fragrant valley in the world, the valley of roses, of antiquities, and of heroes.

BULGARIA COMES ALIVE

For most people as for the writer geography only becomes a living subject when they have travelled in a country; visionary map-voyagers are the rare and fortunate exceptions. I have therefore given it the very minimum space, just sufficient to situate the Bulgarian and to stress the smallness of his living space and numbers. With history it is altogether a different matter.

In France, Joan of Arc and Napoleon still live, an incentive to action, but the taking of the Bastille is only an excuse for dancing in the streets. In England we have obviously been formed by Magna Carta, the Armada, Cromwell, the Bill of Rights and every other event in our long history, but it is only on very special commemorative occasions that we are at all aware of this. The average teenager in this country only felt on one day, the day of the funeral, what Churchill had meant to his parents, and this is no reflection on teenagers. The key to Churchill's greatness was that he was the exception, a man with a sense of history and the obligation due to it. The Bulgarian has this sense of history.

Our street names commemorate landlords, Nelson is a lofty and solitary exception, his square brings to mind bloated pigeons and street photographers rather than a battle.

I had not been in Sofia one morning before I realised that this is completely different with the Bulgarians. I was soon aware that I was among the most history-conscious, history-living people I had ever met. It is in fact impossible to talk to anyone, peasant or professor, for any length of time without some historical allusion. It is impossible to understand the Bulgarians, even superficially, without knowing something of their history. Bulgaria's Pantheon is all around one, in the streets, in the valleys and on the mountains, in universities, schools and kindergartens. Museums are living and consequently invigorating places. Give a cheer for your favourite football teams, Levski, Botev, Rakovski and you are chanting the name of a national hero, climb a mountain and you meet another, stop by the roadway and there is a tablet. Sing a song, recite a poem, read a novel; all are sagas.

If our story began in September 1944 with the communist régime, this could be easily understood; it might be regarded as a propaganda drive. In Bulgaria this is not the case; communist heroes and personalities take their places as the uninterrupted and logical continuation of history; Dimitrov, hero of Leipzig and fighter of fascism, Liliana Dimitrova the inspired and inspiring heroine of the resistance follow hot on the heels of Rakovski, Botev and Levski, fighters of the Turks. I met them all. Time plays curious tricks; fact and bardic legend, recorded history, tradition and myth, all come together in an atmosphere that is so creative and invigorating that it makes a small nation great. Nor is this an alienating Chauvinism or a chip-on-the-shoulder aggressiveness or a desire, by standing on tiptoe, to make what is small seem great. These heroes represent true ideals, they are builders, their example inspires, their virtues are human and always enriched by the hearty rumble of Bulgarian laughter.

I made a comparison with our own reactions to history. No comparison is valid. I do not suggest that our basic patriotism is less, though possibly since the time of Hereward the Wake it may have grown a trifle anaemic! The reason that Bulgaria is taking in history with every breath is due to very special circumstances. Bulgaria was the Sleeping Beauty whose living began again after five centuries of troubled sleep, often of nightmare, punctuated by brief awakenings, the wink of an eyelid, the twitching of a muscle. In 1878, within the memory of a few ancients still alive in a land of many nonagenarians, life started once again. The Odyssey and the Iliad are tales told by grandparents who lived them as children or heard them from their parents and grandparents. There is still this sense of wonder and of a special destiny that a handful of people, mainly peasants, could survive five centuries of occupation that was not only brutal in the extreme but that attempted to obliterate the very sense of identity, encouraging ignorance and corrupting where it did not exterminate.

MILESTONES

I wrote that the total consciousness of the identity of the nation began in 1878. This is not altogether correct. The brief awakenings I mentioned are important, even though they affected a minority. We shall meet many of these heroes in our travels, not as street names or inscriptions on a gravestone but as living people. 'He who falls in battle, fighting for freedom, he does not die . . .' wrote the poet Hristo Botev, who was himself to disappear in battle.

The earliest history of Bulgaria belongs to the archaeologists; Thrace, Greece, Rome and Byzantium are constantly revealing themselves, not only adding to knowledge but to the national consciousness. During my last stay, and I watched it day by day, a handsome Roman mosaic was emerging from the dust behind the largest hotel in Sofia, lovingly uncovered by a group of students and experts. So keen are the authorities on prehistory that an important industrial development has recently been diverted to preserve some remnants of antiquity.

The Bulgarian State was founded in 681 when the proto-Bulgarians, a Turkic tribe from central Asia, in alliance with a union of seven Slav tribes, defeated the Byzantine emperor throwing his army back into the Balkan mountains. The proto-Bulgarians under their leader Asparouh, were predominant and the name Bulgaria* was imposed on the new State and has remained. The process of assimilation of the two peoples lasted several centuries until finally the proto-Bulgarians were assimilated and became Slavs. Under a succession of aggressive Khans, Bulgarian territory expanded at the expense of the Byzantines and by the first half of the ninth century had absorbed a fresh and numerous Slav element. Bulgaria has assimilated the local heritage of the Thracian, Roman and Byzantine eras and this, as I have indicated, is still a continuing process as the spade reveals evidences of these cultures.

Two events are of outstanding importance and must be underlined as ever present in the consciousness of most Bulgarians.

* It is suggested that the words 'Bulgaria' and 'Volga' are connected

The first, in 865, was the introduction under Boris I of Christianity in its Eastern Orthodox form. This meant that Bulgaria could from then on be accepted as a member of the family of Christian states, that the civilisation of Byzantium spread and that its painting, architecture and literature were now indigenous. Christianity also became a common ground between proto-Bulgarians and Slavs and led to the complete assimilation of the proto-Bulgarians and the predominance of the Slav tongue.

The other outstanding event of this period was the appearance of the Slav alphabet and the birth of a national literature.

The Slav alphabet was the invention of the brother saints, Cyril and Methodius, born in Salonica of Slav origin. It was compiled in 855 and became the Cyrillic alphabet. When the brothers were persecuted by the German clergy, three of their disciples found refuge in Bulgaria, bringing with them the precious alphabet and founding a school in which they trained over three thousand five hundred pupils as priests and educators. Bulgaria became the centre of Slav culture and learning. This is as great a source of pride as the possession of Homer to the Greeks. In both cases it was a taxi driver who first stressed this proud heritage. A London taxi driver, salt of the earth, has yet to mention Shakespeare.

These brothers are no longer venerated as saints by the majority but they are very much a source of special pride in the minds of the people. Their statues abound, their image is on postage stamps and schools are named after them. They bore witness for Dimitrov in the Leipzig dock.

In the first quarter of the tenth century Bulgaria reached the height of her expansion and power. The prince (*Knyaz*) Simeon was proclaimed Tsar of the Bulgarians and Greeks; the head of the Church became Patriarch of Bulgaria.

The literature produced at this time was rich in religious, legal and scientific knowledge. Slavonic teaching influenced Bulgaria's neighbours, the Kiev Russians in particular. Many cities, among them Serdica (Sofia today), Plovdiv (the ancient Phillipopolis) and Varna (originally Odessos) became important centres of trade and communication.

Then came a time of continuous warfare against Byzantine and

Tartar invaders and of peasant revolt against Boyar oppression. This coincided with the Bogomolist heresy, named after its founder, Father Bogomil. The Bogomils were dualists, like the Cathari and Albigenses whom they inspired. It was to leave its influence as a popular movement of revolt long after the heresy had disappeared, if in fact it ever has disappeared. It became the spearhead of the revolt against the Byzantines, who were the first to

occupy Bulgaria and began the sturdy breed of resistance fighters who figure in history until 1945.

There were further brief periods of victory and greatness and of a new Bulgarian kingdom when for a time the Byzantines were hurled back. In the thirteenth and fourteenth centuries there was the remarkable cultural flowering that is Bulgaria's special pride at the present day. There are the churches still standing in Turnovo, with their richly decorated frescoes, there is the Rila monastery, for centuries centre of Bulgarian learning under its pious founder, St John of Rila. The supreme monument of medieval art is the

Boyana Church, on the slopes of Vitosha near Sofia. The frescoes here, painted in 1259, a few years before the birth of Giotto, the work of a great unknown master, show the first humanistic trend in painting. The images of the patrons of the church, the boyar Kaloyan and his wife Dessislava, are living portraits and no longer conventional Byzantine images. In many of these portraits we can see the Bulgarian of our time. The last supper is a picture of the life that the artist saw around him. There is a long napkin on the knees of the disciples, and garlic, a popular relish then as now, lies on the table among the dishes. Boyana is the pride of all Bulgarians. We shall visit here and at Rila in a later chapter.

Now comes the long nightmare. Weakened by the continual struggle with Byzantium and split into three warring factions, Bulgaria was finally occupied by the Turks in 1396 after half a century of stubborn resistance.

The people are tortured and made a subject race, the country becomes the personal property of the sultans. Children are carried off and forcibly converted. Buildings are destroyed, paintings mutilated, books burnt. Culture goes underground, kept alive by the monks teaching the people in cell schools, isolated monasteries and troglodyte dwellings. The national Church, expression of the people's identity, is put into the hands of the Greek Patriarchate and the Greeks too become oppressors. Bulgarian emigrants to neighbouring countries keep the flame burning. There is a bold and unsuccessful rising in north Bulgaria in 1598 under Shishman III, proclaimed Tsar as a descendant of the last dynasty. It was the first mass attempt at liberation.

The second renaissance begins in 1762 when the monk Païssi of Hilendar on Mount Athos completed his *Slav-Bulgarian History*. He wrote of the great work of the brother saints Cyril and Methodius and of the valour of Bulgarian arms. He rebuked those who were ashamed to call themselves Bulgarians and who were completely under the influence of Greek education and culture; the subjection of the Church to Greece was a blow second only to that of the Ottoman occupation.

'For the simple Bulgarians,' wrote Païssi, 'I have written it

отиога сия мила моя майно льбо зора ухорил оттодез ся и мила мои майно льбо войска пробырвел

simply.' It was spread far and wide in manuscript, not a book but a deed.

Modern Bulgaria may be said to have begun, it was at any rate the beginning of the beginning, with Païssi's simple history book.

The history of the next hundred years belongs largely to the *haidouti*, those extraordinary men and sometimes women who, goaded beyond endurance, left their homes and went into the mountains where they harried not only the Turks but also the *chorbadjis*, pot-bellied collaborators who had come to terms with the enemy. The *haidouti* are the subject of plays, novels, operas and folk-songs. It is impossible to travel a mile in Bulgaria without meeting these 'patriotic brigands, genuine Robin Hoods', and I stress the comparison a century after it was made by an American missionary because it is still a current one. Robin Hood is a popular character on television, known to every child as 'the English *haidouk*'.

The Bulgarians saw a real hope of freedom in the worsening relations between their Slav brother, Russia, and Turkey, leading to the war in 1768–1774, one of the long series. The population supported the advance of the Russians in north Bulgaria and the great Suvorov commanded Bulgarian guerrilla detachments. I have lunched in the delightful village of Suvorov, where the general's portrait hangs in a place of honour in the cooperative farm's amateur artist's exhibition room – every worker knew his history and was proud of the association. Their hopes from this war were premature, but it was the beginning of the end, an end long drawn out by Napoleon's invasion of Russia, Russia's defeat in the Crimean War and the tortuous politics of the great powers who tried to keep the mouldering Turkish Empire alive as a counterweight to Russia.

Parallel with this movement for political independence there was the fierce struggle for ecclesiastical freedom against the Turkish imposed Greek metropolitans. 'The Sultan could never have crushed the heart out of his Christian subjects without the aid of a Christian middleman and the Greek has used the brute force of his Mohammedan employer to complement his own cleverness and guile,' wrote an English traveller in 1867. This fight, the training ground for resistance, which has its significance to the present day, was won in 1870, eight years before independence.[*]

The Turks grew weaker, more corrupt and more brutal, the *Bashi-bazouks* and Circassians crushing the peasant risings, slaughtering men, women and children and burning villages with a sadistic thoroughness not to be seen again until the Nazi destruction of Oradour and Lidice.

The 1860's mark the peak period of organised resistance, led in many cases by poets who were men of action, till in 1876 came the uprising that was one of the greatest episodes in Bulgarian history; tragic, reckless, ill planned and doomed from the start, yet so magnificent that it turned the eyes of the world on Bulgaria. It was

---

[*] Officially the schism ended in 1945, when the Greek Patriarchate recognised the independence of the Bulgarian Church.

repressed with such savagery that the civilised world was horrified; Tolstoy, Dostoievsky, Victor Hugo, Darwin, Oscar Wilde raised their voices in protest. Gladstone made his famous series of speeches on Bulgarian atrocities. He is remembered in Bulgaria today, perhaps more than in England. I certainly heard his name mentioned more in a week than in twenty years at home. The good-will is not yet exhausted.

The Russo-Turkish War of 1877 and the victories at Shipka and Pleven finally brought independence in 1878 with the Treaty of San Stefano. This was not quite the end of the story. The Congress of Berlin, with its hypocritical and sordid slogan of 'Peace with Honour', postponed complete victory for a few years. Bulgaria was carved into three parts, Macedonia being tossed back to the Turks, and was given an alien ruler, a German princeling, which was to bring further distress and much bloodshed.

This has been a breathless survey of a long and complex history, necessarily incorrect because of the many omissions. It has, how-ever, been absolutely necessary not only as a background to the characters and places we shall come across but because it is essen-tial for any understanding of Bulgaria today. It throws a strong light in particular on three points: the State's attitude to the Church as distinct from religion, the very special relationship with Russia, the inevitability and the suitability of a communist people's republic.

THE ATTITUDE TO RELIGION

The Bulgarian constitution postulates, 'both the freedom of conscience and religion and the right to perform religious rites and ceremonies. The socialist state considers religion as a personal matter. Every citizen may profess any religion, provided that he does no harm to others and does not endanger public order.'

Some such clause is written into many constitutions and easily forgotten; in Bulgaria I believe it to be a fact. There is absolutely no hatred of the Church, because in the struggle for ecclesiastical freedom the priests were for the most part on the same side as the people and against the wealthy who had compromised, because since the time of Cyril and Methodius churchmen had been pioneers of popular education, because of the monk Païssi's stirring call to the people, because Pope André manned a gun in the anti-fascist September rising of 1923 and became a folk hero. In Russia, on the contrary, the Church that excommunicated Tolstoy had always been associated with Tsarism, obscurantism and oppression.

'Our Church,' Dr Peter Voutov, Minister of Culture, told me, 'has always been progressive. Even when Bulgaria was allied with Germany against communist Russia not more than a handful of priests collaborated with the enemy. We do not believe in persecution from any point of view, neither do we as communists believe in religion. I think that with education it will gradually fade away. In the meantime, if some people feel the need for religion, the State maintains it, paying the salaries of the Orthodox Church, the Mohammedans, Jews and Armeno-Gregorians, subsidising the theological faculty and restoring and maintaining a number of churches and cathedrals. If you like, I could introduce you to a bishop but the best thing for you to do would be to meet a village priest and hear what he has to say.' Later I had a talk with an English-speaking monk met at random. He confirmed that there was absolutely no persecution, though the whole bias of education was naturally anti-religious and it was having its effect, young people were not coming to church. He went on, 'although, for different reasons and by a different road, this State has achieved a remarkable measure of social justice of which I as a Christian approve.'

Recently, when some hooligans, with a missionary zeal not unworthy of Mr Kensit and his followers, tried to interrupt an Easter service, they were forcibly removed by the militia* and severely punished. The episode was told me by a member of the congregation.

Communists do not shun the Church or regard it with horror; they appreciate its aesthetic and cultural values and occasionally visit it to hear the music. In cities and villages there are as many priests to be seen as in any non-communist state; and remarkably impressive they are, long haired and bearded like the prophets, stove-pipe hatted and with raven robes flowing.

* In Bulgaria the word 'police' is tainted and 'militia' used in the sense of our police.

BULGARIAN-RUSSIAN FRIENDSHIP

The reason for the friendship with Russia, intellectual and emotional, is again obvious from the history I have outlined. The Russians alone held out against the rest of Europe for Bulgarian independence. There is a tower at Shipka that celebrates the successful defence of the pass by a mixed detachment of Bulgarians and Russians. There are two other monuments to Russian arms in Sofia, the impressive equestrian statue of the liberating Tsar Alexander II, erected in 1907, and the monument 'to the Soviet Army of freedom from the grateful people of Bulgaria', erected in 1945. The Alexander Nevsky cathedral, the focal point of Sofia, was built by popular subscription in memory of the Russian soldiers who had died for Bulgaria. There are the museums all over Bulgaria that celebrate Bulgarian–Russian friendship. In Bulgaria monuments are not merely roosting places for pigeons but places for pious reflection. Nor are they ever taken for granted.

This then is no product of Soviet communist propaganda but a manifestation of the peoples' kinship and gratitude both pre- and post-revolutionary. The Bulgarians do not regard themselves as satellites – we have seen their intense feeling of identity throughout the century – but as friends.* The might of the USSR reassures but does not overawe them; in a sense they see themselves as equal partners, the eight million with the two hundred million. It is true politically that, if Russia catches cold Bulgaria sneezes, but since Stalin there is more and more the realisation that there is the Bulgarian way of doing things, especially in the field of education.

THE PEOPLE'S REPUBLIC

Finally, the history that I have outlined shows that the present régime in Bulgaria is not the result of external aggression nor of a sudden revolution. It is an evolution, foreshadowed in Bogomil times.† The wealthy man, the *chorbadji*, was for centuries identified

* In an article in *The Times* of November the fourteenth, 1965, entitled 'Bulgaria Opens Door to West' the eastern European correspondent writes of the *myth* of absolute loyalty and eternal gratitude to Russia and calls it an anachronism. It is no myth but very much of a reality for the reasons I have shown

† The Bogomil movement was a theological one. It has, however, been adopted by Marxist historians for the resistance it showed to the authority of the ruling class.

with the enemy and an alien way of life, and the peasant and the poet, singer of the people's songs, with resistance and patriotism. The symbol of resistance was not a prince but a *haidouk*, who found refuge and comfort in the peasant's hut and the poor monk's cell. When a monarchy was imposed from outside, a totally alien conception, it had little meaning in reason or emotion. The Bulgarian was a natural born socialist before he became a philosophical socialist. In 1923, he was the first to rise up, at frightful cost, against the fascist movement, supported only by Soviet Russia. It was in Russia that the Bulgarian workers' movement, weak and divided at first, found its original strength. Dimiter Blagoev, a pioneer in Russia of Marxist organisation, went on to form the Bulgarian Social Democratic Party. Bulgarian communists were trained and worked alongside the first Russian communists. After the Russian October Revolution it was merely a matter of time until the Bulgarians followed suit. When, in 1940, the ruling classes, a small minority, for the second time formed an unnatural alliance with Germany against Russia, doing violence to the deepest emotional feelings of the people, their fate was sealed.

It is only right to say that the 1944 revolution took place in the presence of the Soviet army, shocking and surprising the Western Powers. As in the past the West had always used Bulgaria as a pawn in power politics, it is reasonable to doubt whether it could have exercised any influence in what was a natural evolution. The exact number of people killed, apart from active Nazi collaborators, is not easy to come by. It was a comparatively bloodless revolution. During the later Stalinist days there were a number of innocent victims.

Whatever one's view of communism, in Bulgaria of all countries it is a natural phenomenon that today satisfies the aspirations of the overwhelming majority of the people. I have heard certain members of the government strongly criticised as individuals, I have found actions of the government criticised and freely so, but no one has anything but pride in the achievement of the past twenty years or wishes to put the clock back.

3. SOFIA

At the time of the liberation and for twenty years after, when *The Times* correspondent J. D. Bouchier first came to love it, Sofia was a picturesque and squalid oriental town of twenty thousand inhabitants. Some years before Lamartine had dismissed it in a paragraph. Ox carts creaked over the uneven Turkish cobbles; sanitary conditions and comfort, as a European knows them, hardly existed outside the Prince's Palace. Thereafter its growth was rapid, though its centre was largely destroyed by allied air raids in the last war. Today it is a modern capital with some seven hundred thousand inhabitants, having doubled its population in under twenty years. In another twenty years it should have a million and a half. There is the space and new building is flourishing.

Its beauty is greater than the sum total of its buildings and monuments. It is the perfect garden city with over three hundred parks and one hundred thousand trees. The biggest of all, The Park of Freedom, has a thousand acres of pine forest, lawns, flower-beds, a swimming-pool and an agricultural research station. It nestles eighteen hundred feet above sea level under the seven-thousand-foot Mount Vitosha, the friendly mountain, Sofia's nursing mother. In the past it sheltered the partisans, today it is a picnic ground in summer and in winter a sports resort, an inexpensive twenty minute bus ride from the centre of the city. On a fine Sunday Sofia is emptied as almost the whole population finds its way there. Various groups of workers have their chalets, parties of volunteers make or tend the roads and paths. Ruskin would have approved. Its natural beauty has been enhanced by the planting of flowers, trees and shrubs, leading one gently into the virgin forest. Cafés, restaurants and chalets have been skilfully designed to blend with the scenery. Sofia seen at night from Vitosha gains a beauty that suddenly transforms it into a wonder city; the lights seen through a heat haze become a milky way, the car headlights, shooting stars and the golden domes of Alexander Nevsky, brilliant planets.

Sofia is not a tourist city in the sense of Rome, Venice, Florence, Paris, Leningrad or Amsterdam. It can be seen in two days, it reveals itself slowly. Its genial charm grew on me, it is a place to live in and to stroll in, the cosy garden city to which to return. I smile as I think of my next visit.

My mother always maintained that one could recognise certain cities blindfolded. In her favourite, Paris, there was a very special Gare du Nord aroma and the *pah-poum* of the motor horns, no longer sounded, gave it a very definite signature tune. In Sofia it is the heavy aromatic scent of the linden trees and the smell of roses in the flower-beds, massed in parks and on the road verges, the rustle of leaves in the trees and a bird song as loud and musical as in any woodland clearing. Paustovsky begins his essay on Bulgaria by commenting on this characteristic sound. In Russia, he says, *shoum* means noise, in Bulgaria foliage is *shouma*, how right this is, the leaves are constantly in motion.

When one opens one's eyes the predominant colour is green, trees everywhere and parks where mothers, fathers and grandparents take their babies for an airing, little girls run around with their stiff plastic bows bobbing. Old ladies with heads bound in black kerchiefs sit round a fountain knitting and exchanging gossip. One comes across groups of laughing people who greet one another in the street, transforming the city into a village. There are big modern buildings and dotted among them shaded retreats of antiquity, piously preserved, such as the Roman baths and the fourth-century church of St George nestling in the courtyard of the grandiose Balkan Hotel. Two unobtrusive churches I remember in particular. Outside the Rila Hotel, and so dwarfed by it that it looks like a building-site hut, is the Church of St George. It has no artistic merit, the previous church was destroyed in the bombing but it is deeply moving. It seems to cling to life so precariously. On its site there had been a jeweller's shop belonging to a certain Georgi, a handsome man and a noted singer. He was 'invited' by the Turks to turn Moslem, refused and was martyred in 1515.

Another appealing church in the centre of the city is the Holy Friday Church of the donkey-harness makers. It is a fifteenth-century building erected over a seventh-century church that had been built over a second-century pagan temple.

Let us take a leisurely stroll, as I did on that first morning, without the encumbrance of a fixed sightseeing programme. That can wait; there is enough of the oriental in the Bulgarian to justify such procrastination. In any case during our half-hour stroll we shall learn more about Bulgaria than in many weeks on the Black Sea Riviera that is so urgently summoning the tourist by rail, coach and plane.

At most times of the day the streets in the centre are as crowded and as animated as in southern France, Spain or Italy. There is no feeling of regimentation or strain, people are well but not fashionably dressed. From time to time near the big hotels there are two or three very dark-skinned gypsy women, with fine-cut Hindu features, and these are the only beggars I have ever seen in any communist country. People look upon them with tolerant disapproval. 'They have never been politically conscious and never will be. They are mostly dishonest but they have always been a part of the landscape and always will.' I hope so; only in Spain have I seen such magnificent gypsy faces.

The Bulgarians are a handsome race, 'stalwart, beautiful people,' wrote Tolstoy. What distinguishes them from all other peoples is the extraordinary beauty of their eyes. They are large and splendidly formed, fringed by long lashes, very bright and varying in colour from black to green. Unlike those large limpid liquid oriental eyes, celebrated by eastern poets, they are never bovine. They show intelligence and humour. Every Bulgarian has at the corner of the eyes and mouth the creases of smiles ready to turn into hearty laughter. I pointed this out to a Bulgarian friend who was so fascinated by the discovery that for a time we stood on the animated Boulevard Rouski peering at faces. My case was proved. I could always recognise a Bulgarian by the eyes.

The shop windows show a wide variety of consumer goods; refrigerators, television sets, radiograms, transistors, cameras, watches, winter sports and beach outfits and articles of clothing. There are large stores with attractive displays and small specialist shops. Though all are State owned these small shops have a personality, and the shopkeepers are eager to please.

The bookshops are especially tempting and always attract a crowd; large editions of a new book may be sold out in a day. Bookshops are of two kinds, those that specialise in Bulgarian books and those selling foreign books, mainly Russian; the Russian books are cheaper than in Russia itself. I noticed, and not only in Sofia, a large number of English works published in Russia; *Lorna Doone*, the works of Oscar Wilde, *The Man of Property*, *The Egoist*, American books by Sinclair Lewis, Mark Twain, Theodore Dreiser and Frank Norris and books by the Australian, Dymphna Cusak. In all the bookshops there are large sections devoted to educational and technical works and also to the communist classics. Photographs of Marx, Lenin, Blagoev, Kolarov and Dimitrov are permanently on view. The Bulgarian bookshops carry many English translations published by the Foreign Languages Press, very well done and splendidly produced. They range from 'boost' books, indigestible, statistic-laden and, if propagandist, liable to defeat their object in a society where the achievement is all around one, to scholarly and well edited books dealing with the country's art treasures and works of serious literary interest that deserve a far wider audience than that of the casual tourist, whose baggage space is limited and who is probably no great reader. Books, the theatre, and food are the cheapest of all commodities, within reach of the poorest. This People's Republic has a true sense of priorities.

For the tourist the most inviting shops of all are those with the sign of 'the eye on the outstretched hand' which are run by the Association of Bulgarian artists. They sell more than the customary tourist souvenirs that so soon find their way to the jumble sale or the attic; the ceramics are especially attractive, there are admirable replicas of antique jewellery, fine leather work, wood carving, embroidery and metal work, none of which is fussily folksy. There are also some highly stylised and brightly coloured dolls with a suggestion of national costume. There is one little figure of a bushy moustached peasant astride a small donkey. This is Sly Peter (*Hitur Peter*), a folk hero, Bulgaria's Tyl Eulenspiegel. He scores off all his neighbours and particularly off the Turkish occupants. He has been filmed and turned into opera. Here are some typical Sly Peterisms.

In the village where Peter lived there was a shrew, ill-natured, foul-tongued and neglectful of her duties. Her malignant influence spread quickly over the village. So one day Peter went to the *cadi* (Turkish magistrate) and said, 'We must do something about that woman. She fouls the air of our village.'

'Every man for himself,' replied the *cadi*, 'if she is lazy and disreputable, that's her own business.'

So Sly Peter went home, killed one of his goats and hooked it on the door. After a few days it began to rot and the villagers complained to the *cadi* that it was fouling the air and might spread disease. The *cadi* summoned Peter and told him to dispose of the nuisance.

'Every man for himself,' said Peter. 'It is my goat and my business what I do with it.'

On another occasion a rich man slapped Peter on the face for some slight offence. Peter got very angry and went to the *cadi* to complain. The *cadi* said, 'Don't complain, Peter, he is a wealthy man. Today he'll slap you on the face and tomorrow he'll give you a piece of gold.'

'Oh, if a slap on the face is worth a piece of gold, here you are,' and Peter slapped the *cadi* on the face.

'Now I owe you a piece of gold and as you are on such good terms with the rich man he'll pay you the piece of gold he owes me. Now we're quits.'

Sly Peter, astride his donkey rests, on my desk.

All these objects are inexpensive, admired by the Bulgarians as well as the tourists. Very expensive are the copies of ikons, sometimes limited to one. Brought back home, these could certainly be sold as originals and most probably are.

Every hotel has a souvenir counter and also a display window with more luxury goods, fur coats and the like, only sold for foreign currency. There are also the foreign currency *Corecom* shops filled with imported goods. It is a sign of the maturity of the people that, though they naturally covet some of these rare articles, they understand their country's need for foreign currency. There has been criticism but I have never heard a grumble. In fact many of these, to us familiar articles, were in no way superior to the locally produced ones, though they were more attractively packaged.

In the stationers' shops there are postcards of familiar faces. Laurence Olivier can be seen everywhere and, in such a Shakespeare-conscious country, is really well known. But by far the most popular English personality is 'Mr Pitkin', mentioned to me by everyone I met. It was only when I saw a cinema poster that I identified him as Norman Wisdom. One is lamentably ignorant of one's ambassadors.

Posted on the walls one sees, as in Italy, obituary notices headed by photographs of the deceased, only far more numerous since the newspapers do not carry obituaries. These interested me particularly, as some carried the conventional cross while others had the hammer and sickle; a few were uncommitted.

At one street corner there is always a crowd watching the large display windows outside the American Legation. Next door, as an antidote, a photographer's shop has its windows full of Soviet and other communist material. On the first occasion that I passed, the Americans had a window of exceptionally dull photographs devoted to the life of Duke Ellington and another, very well set out,

1. Welcoming Russian soldiers in Svishtov. June 15, 1877

2. Welcoming of the Russian soldiers in Sofia, 1944

3. St George's Church in the courtyard of Hotel Balkan

4. The Alexander Nevsky Cathedral in Sofia

to their recent space achievement. The communist retort was also a series of cosmonaut pictures, giving high praise to the Americans but featuring a chart that showed that the record was at that time still held by the USSR. The other window was devoted to the American aggression in Vietnam, a trump card. I watched the crowd as keenly as the windows. They showed a quiet but unmistakably positive reaction. It is well to remember that here Vietnam is looked upon with very much the same horror [justifiably, I believe, as by an increasing number of Americans themselves] as our Left looked on Franco's Spanish Civil War. The next time I was in Sofia, the Americans devoted a whole window to a young dancer who had failed to pass into the second round of the Varna contest and who obviously did not particularly distinguish herself. The communists did not retort with pictures of the many Soviet gold medallists but with a painful series of photographs of the Gerald Brooke trial in Moscow and further scenes from Vietnam. The second American window consisted of tractors, irrigation and factories. This last could have belonged to both worlds and it attracted some interest. Surely these rival windows are a healthy sign of the agreement to disagree.

The Bulgarians are essentially tolerant. Oppression has taught them not to oppress. Their record with the Jewish minority is exceptional, as Hannah Arendt testifies, and not only for that part of the world. Like the Danes and many Italians they refused, in spite of strong pressure, to hand over their Jews to the Nazis. Dimitrov, alone among communist leaders, allowed Jews to emigrate to Israel, whose relations with Bulgaria are particularly good. In spite of five centuries of history the Turkish minority is exceptionally well treated. When the Turkish radio put out alarming rumours of a possible drive against the Turks many wished to emigrate. They were immediately granted exit visas. Later when the majority wanted to return they were readmitted without delay; a thoroughly adult attitude at once humane and excellent propaganda. I noticed that in the Varna competition a Turkish entrant received a particularly warm and neighbourly welcome as did the Greek contestants.

This Bulgarian tolerance is not caused by apathy or indifference.

c

It is ingrained in the national character and is revealed in every attitude. It is also fostered by the authorities as a policy of wisdom in a small country. As early as 1867 an English traveller wrote: 'The Bulgarians are wise rather than clever' – a very shrewd observation. On many occasions I commented on the absence of foreign non-communist papers in the street kiosks; unlike in Russia, they are provided free for tourists in the holiday resort hotels. The reply, which had some measure of truth, was that whenever Bulgaria was mentioned it was in a negative sense. For instance, the reports of political unrest in the spring of 1965, an unrest not noticed by the ordinary Bulgarian (no one I knew had been affected) cost them many tourist cancellations. They also considered that the western Press included too many trivialities and showed a false set of values. 'At home you are able,' I was told, 'to read more than one paper, you are familiar with their tendencies and weigh one against the other.' This was not merely an excuse brought up for the occasion. The western Press is available in the libraries for serious language students for whom there is no ban on foreign books, as I saw from the list of recommended reading given to university students; it included Evelyn Waugh and other non-communist contemporaries as well as Dickens, the Brontës and other classics. I have since sent many books to my friends and all have been received.

For weeks I never tired of roaming the Sofia streets, picking up casual acquaintances, which was only too easy as I had made a number of television appearances, given interviews and written in the Press. On one of the very first days my wife asked the way of a young man. He was a student, answered her in fluent Russian and accompanied us part of the way. A few days later he found us at our hotel and invited us to supper with his family. It was our first visit to a Bulgarian home. The supper was lavish, the wines well chosen, the family altogether enchanting. The father was an old party man, an active revolutionary and an intellectual who had been a refugee in Russia during the fascist days and who had married a Russian wife. He had been through everything, the fascist persecution at home and the Stalinist terror in the USSR.

'In many ways,' he said, 'it was less bad than at home. Our

greatest failing is envy. We are a small country, everyone knows what his neighbour is doing, we are an ambitious people. Moscow was big enough for anonymity and people stuck together. In those days, and they were bad days, unless you had the misfortune to be prominent you could get by.' They all agreed that envy was a Bulgarian failing, the result of long years of poverty. I asked him if things had worked out the way he wanted. He was emphatic in his answer. 'The Balkans were once a byword for unrest and anarchic conditions. We warred amongst our neighbours, there was no security or stability at home. The great powers, who played us one against the other for motives of their own, said that we were a wild people and that it was our nature to be fighters. Twice in my life-time a government under an alien monarch arbitrarily flouted the will of the people and made us fight against our Russian brothers. Now the people rule. Look at us, the most peaceful and peace-loving part of the world. We live in security, our government has just signed a treaty of friendship with Greece and relations have never been better. Incidentally, neither Greeks nor Turks live as comfortably or as amicably together as we do with our neighbours. Turkish illiteracy is as high as 50 per cent, ours has been wiped out. Look at the rest of the world, the Americas for instance. They might well envy the peace of the Balkans, if they learnt to think objectively. That is what we communists have fought for, peace, justice and security.'

Yes, he was well satisfied now, lived comfortably on his pension, his wife was still of working age and they were able to give their children the best of educations.

In every conversation, with all types of people, the very first thing to be stressed was the education of the children, not only in a narrow technical speciality but in languages and the arts. In this they resembled the Scots. They were frugal, their needs were not great, books were a prime necessity. Only in the entertainment of the stranger did they spend without stint.

As well as the student son, our original friend, there was a schoolgirl daughter who spoke excellent English. The daughter was politically inclined like her father and very well informed, the son mainly interested in his special field, the mother a homemaker concerned in preserving harmony, not too difficult in a tolerant country where family ties are exceptionally strong, where in spite of the equality of women and the paternal role of the State, the father is looked up to in his own home. In any case, Bulgarian conversation usually ends in a laugh. Suddenly I felt myself back in England, in Bath or Cheltenham at an earlier age, with the party member in the role of the Conservative paterfamilias. It was not the last time I was to feel this particular atmosphere in a family. It surprised me at first to equate the old revolutionary with the Edwardian paterfamilias, listened to with respect by his family. I wish others could enjoy this revealing experience of 'one man's orthodoxy . . .' We stayed till after one in the morning.

Walking home that night I saw a militiaman dragging off an irate young man with a pretty girl standing crying by his side. In a few seconds a small crowd gathered. The couple had been caught in a too affectionate embrace and apparently the boy had expressed his opinion of the militia with some frankness. The sympathy of the crowd was obviously with the lovers. I told a friend of this incident and his reaction was the same. 'Damn the police. Who would enter such a profession? They are the same the world over.' I told him that we did not think of our police in that way. He was sceptical. 'Who are you kidding? I tell you they are all the same. I read all about it in your *Daily Worker*.' I told him that the Challenor case was exceptional and that Parliament and Press often curbed the police to such an extent that the criminal was the gainer. He shrugged his shoulders in disbelief. Was this a hangover from the fascist and Stalinist days or the usual continental hatred of the *flic?*

I cannot answer the obvious question at this stage how far is this a police state, though I feel sure that today no one is imprisoned for the private expression of his opinions. I only met one suspicious character, a man and his wife who joined our table when my wife and I were dining alone, helped us with the menu and then started to show considerable curiosity. I found him completely ignorant of his alleged profession and more than embarrassed by the questions I put to him. He may have been made suspicious by the copious notes I was taking; about food, incidentally. He left the restaurant without paying and was shown a certain respect. If he was in fact a security man, he was a remarkably stupid one and was certainly exceeding his authority, since my visit was no secret. He may have been checking up on the conduct of tourists in general, as he was full of information about numbers and nationalities. From my point of view his saving grace was a very beautiful wife, his valuable advice about wine and a love of good food. I took some photographs for the sake of her looks and he was in no way disconcerted.

Many people lived in picturesque old style two or three storeyed ivy- or vine-covered houses that had belonged to their parents. The authorities had allowed them to stay on after the revolution but had rationed the rooms. Now more families lived in the house, usually relatives; the house-owner could choose his co-inhabitant. Most of them had their names down for big modern flats and the houses seemed so cosy and attractive that I was surprised until I came to realise the serious heating problems and the increased work that was the price to pay for the picturesque. The flats, often in a large complex, compared favourably with modern flats in any city, they had large balconies and were situated among gardens with ample playing space for the children and room for parking prams. As in many Italian buildings the lifts required a coin to operate them; the sum was negligible, the inconvenience great for the absent-minded who lived on the eleventh floor.

One thing I very soon noticed in the streets and parks of Sofia and other big cities was the almost total absence of dogs; a contrast to our own fouled pavements. The general view was that they should only be kept when the owner had sufficient private ground to exercise them. The sporting dog in the country was very popular.

I came across a group of Africans, obviously students. (Officially there is no colour bar and, of course, no landlady problem.) They stood out more than at home. Numbers of African students go to Bulgaria, especially for training in medicine and agriculture. A little time ago there was considerable publicity about disquiet among these students and incidents were reported in the Press. Some of the students had apparently objected to the living allowance, more than that granted to the Bulgarians, and others to the necessity of attending classes in dialectical materialism, though this was part of the contract.

The private attitude of the Bulgarian is much the same as that of all liberal-minded people who are also realists; here are lonely foreigners and we must make them welcome, but there are problems, particularly where relationships between the sexes are concerned, and these cannot be brushed aside. These people must be equipped to return to their own countries, taking with them our skills and experience. It is naturally hoped that this will lead them to communism; and it may, but not as surely and directly as Smethwick or Los Angeles. If it does come, it will be something different. A Negro to whom I talked was non-committal. For the present he appreciated the opportunity to learn. He spoke Bulgarian and shared a room with a Bulgarian student. I felt that it was not the indoctrination as much as the conduct of the individual that would count in the long run. The Bulgarian has a tremendous advantage, his country was a colony for half a millennium.

One of the most enchanting places in which to dine out in Sofia is the Russian Restaurant in Dobrouja Street. It is sometimes called the Russian club and it has the atmosphere of a club, being situated in a large private house with an attractive courtyard. The food is extra good, the waiters of the old-fashioned type, fastly disappearing all over the world and, greatest blessing of all, there is no music. Sofia has a night club 'The Astoria', for visitors I imagine, but I stayed away. Even the most conscientious tourist can be excused the smoky boredom of a night club.

People love walking in Sofia and they are untiring. Everything is 'just a short walk'. Part of the charm is in running across friends. I have never walked more in any city or with greater pleasure. One of my most interesting walks was with the head of the protocol department, Alexander Belkovsky, a magnificent looking man, tall and with snow-white hair. I learnt that he was the son of a leading painter and had had an interesting career; when suspected of Marxist tendencies as a student he had gone into exile, working as a docker, a miner, a market porter and a washer-up in France and Belgium. He knew every stone in Sofia, was an archaeological expert and a lover of ecclesiastical art. He spoke in such a rapid flow of French that it was difficult to take notes, which I regret, but the man himself was vastly appealing.

It was with him and through him that I visited a museum that might easily escape attention; the Ecclesiastical Museum. It contained ikons and frescoes, some reproduced and others original. I noted that many of them, otherwise intact, had the eyes defaced. I was told that this arose out of a superstition that to destroy a saint's eyes would restore one's own.

The most beautiful object was a low relief carving of St George, and St Demeter from the tenth century, surrounded by a sixteenth-century painting.

The great value of the museum however was that it contained small models of all the important churches that survived the destruction of over two thousand by the Turks and that I was to see on my journey through the country.

OUTSIDE SOFIA

There is so much to be seen in Sofia that it is tempting to remain. Three excursions should be made. The first, to Borovets, is purely scenic. It is a magnificent mountain resort in the pinewoods at an altitude of four thousand feet. In winter, a sports paradise and in summer an escape from the heat of the plains. It has hotels, many workers' rest homes, a camping ground and some *datchas*. The other two excursions are essential; historically and artistically.

The Rila Monastery situated in a fold of the Rila mountains, the highest in south eastern Europe, nestles in a deep forest of beech and pine. It consists of a huge block of buildings enclosing an irregular rectangular court in the middle of which stands the domed church with its graceful black and white portico and the large square brick tower, Hrelyu's Tower, all that remains from antiquity, and graceful fountains and wellheads. Even this was built in the mid-fourteenth century, three hundred years after the original establishment of the monastery in 927 by John of Rila.

At the foot of the tower is a cell where insane persons were kept until brought into the church for exorcism. This continued as recently as a hundred years ago, when a monk asked that enthusiastic traveller Miss Mackenzie if there were madmen in England.

'Yes,' she replied, 'but instead of cells we lodge them in large and airy dwellings and instead of the priest they are brought to the doctors.'

'And do they recover?'

'They do sometimes, but, alas, not always.'

'Strange,' he replied, 'that is just the same way with ours.'

From the fifteenth to the eighteenth century Rila remained a centre of Bulgarian learning and art, an oasis in a country that was 'behind God's back'. Over the centuries it has been burnt and rebuilt many times, the last time in 1833. The calm beauty of its great colonnades painted with religious and decorative frescoes and its long three-tiered galleries connecting one hundred and seventy-three rooms is dramatically enhanced by the forbidding fortress-like exterior. Once through the gates we step from the Middle Ages to the Renaissance, from arms to learning, from *Macbeth* to *Romeo and Juliet*. It is a picture-book of Bulgarian culture erected at a time when, as Kanitz, an Austrian, wrote, 'no one knew that such a people existed', and an English traveller was surprised to hear the unexpected sound of church bells in the forest. The monastery museum and archives contain not only old Bibles, coins, weapons and church vestments and fragments of the original frescoes, but also a history of Turkish occupation and the struggle for identity and survival. It is no longer used as a monastery and the cells are now guest-rooms.

The mood was completely broken for me when I sat in the café of the Balkantourist hotel, looking at the vast panorama through its large windows. There, where all should have been peace, the jukebox raged, scraped and roared its inanities, a denial of the message of centuries. It should be removed forthwith. And I must add that it was not being fed by the tourists but by some Bulgarian youths.

In a secluded spot outside the monastery there is a close link with England, the tomb of J. D. Bouchier, former Eton master and *The Times* Balkan correspondent. He is lovingly remembered as a staunch friend of Bulgaria. A set of postage stamps bore his portrait.

I have already mentioned the Boyana Church, a few miles from Sofia. It is a small building in cubic form with a graceful cupola rising from its tiled roof. An inscription reads, 'Erected from its foundations this immaculate temple of our Lord's saintly hierarch Nicholas and of Christ's most saintly martyr Pantaleon, with the means, care and great affection of Sebastocrator Kaloyan, cousin of the Tsar and grandson of St Stephen – King of Servie. Frescoed in the Kingdom of Bulgara in the reign of the orthodox, devout and Christ-abiding Tsar Constantine-Assen. Indiction VII of the year 674 (1259).'

On entering this small and unpretentious building I was amazed by the richness of the frescoes depicting some three hundred figures in two small rooms. So skilled is the composition that the effect is never overpowering. In scale and in colour they are perfectly attuned to the architecture, the work of a great and anonymous master. He has succeeded, in spite of the rigorous discipline imposed by the Church, in narrating scenes from the lives of Christ, the Virgin and St Nicholas with a moving realism that predates Giotto. These are portraits of the people he saw around him, embellished with pious imagination. Yet the exciting wealth of detail is always subordinated to the whole. This is surely the greatest work of art to be seen in Bulgaria.

However much one may enjoy street life and excursions, hunger intervenes at the same regular intervals as at home.

4. A SAVOURY INTERLUDE AND SOME PRACTICAL INFORMATION

In my time in Bulgaria I must have eaten some hundreds of meals; in smart tourist hotels, village inns, collective farms and private houses. Some were indeed memorable by any standards, not one was of poor quality and, in spite of the overeating and drinking inevitable in a hospitable country, there were no ill effects.

The breakfast is simple, yoghourt and bread and cheese. For the foreigner there is his usual fare with a dish that I deciphered from the Cyrillic script as *Xemendecks*.* Always ready for a gastronomic novelty I ordered it as a local delicacy but it turned out to be that sublime English discovery, ham and eggs cooked in the familiar manner. Tea is made from bags, imported from England. Coffee is either Turkish or more usually instant. The latter, either for reasons of economy or laziness, is unfortunately replacing one of the few good things introduced under Ottoman rule. It is a singularly characterless drink, though the brand, imported from Israel, seems better than most.

Soups and the heavier fried dishes, cooked in butter or sunflower oil, are to be found in day-time, grills at the evening meal. The *à la carte* menus tend to be uniform in most Balkan tourist hotels, but the variety is enough to give one a change of dish for

---

* I once saw it on a menu followed by the words 'and with eggs' in brackets.

several weeks. There are endless varieties of pork and veal, *schnitzel*, from Vienna to the Bosphorus, brains, kidneys, liver, lamb and chicken. There are many oriental and Russian dishes with a wide choice of Bulgarian specialities. Such delicacies as *Poulet à la Kiev* and roast sucking pig appeared regularly at my favourite restaurant in the Balkan Hotel, whose menu also rang endless changes on risotto, including one recently named for Vietnam, well flavoured with garlic. In restaurants which only serve Bulgarian dishes and where national music is played, a loaf of oven-hot bread called *pitka* and a condiment of incense-like aroma, *choubritsa*, made of dried thyme, pepper and salt make one of the most succulent and the most filling meals I have tasted.

Typical Bulgarian dishes, well spiced and very tasty, are *shoppska* salad, *tarator* soup, *mish-mash, guvech*, various kebabs of minced meats and herbs, an omelet made with white cheese and, of course, the inevitable *Kiselo Mlyako* (yoghourt), either thick or thinned and drunk in a long glass. It has been held to be the prime recipe for longevity ever since the Russian, Dr Mechnikov, wrote his paper on the *bacillus bulgaricus*. He himself did not live to so very great an age.

For myself, I prefer the Bulgarian wine, at its best second only to the vintage wines of France and Germany. I enjoy wine books and small doses of vinous whimsicality but I have not been able to master the jargon and in spite of many tastings in the vineyards, jovial rather than scientific occasions, I can do no more than to recommend. My choice would be the Karlovo Misket not unlike a Sancerre, Dimiat and Château Euxinograd among the white wines, all reasonably dry and grape scented. Among the red, Gumza seems to me outstanding where one would drink a Burgundy. Wine growing is an important industry, good vintage and real quality are appreciated as much as quantity. I suggested to Dr Voutov that wine should be taken over by his Ministry of Culture! The idea was well received. The Bulgarian is a wine drinker but extremely temperate. In all my travels I met but one drunken Bulgarian and he was celebrating some special event with sodden amiability. Drink is no problem in Bulgaria. There are a number of brandies, good but unsubtle, an excellent *marc* and the more popular drinks of *mastika* (the French *pastis*, the Greek *oozo*) and plum brandy, *slivova*. There is also a liqueur made from the famous roses. I cannot recommend it save once, as an experience. For dessert, there are succulent strawberries, raspberries, plums, cherries, peaches and apples and grapes in season. There are some especially good cakes; *garach* (a variety of *Sacher Torte*) and a butter cake with chopped walnuts that is completely irresistible.

For the tourist it is possible to eat well for from seven shillings and sixpence to ten shillings, excessively at over that, and to add a bottle of good wine for five shillings.

A feature of all restaurants is that, unlike the USSR, there are more natives than tourists and the tourists are not given an uncomfortable VIP precedence. Tips of 10 per cent are sometimes given even by Bulgarians but they are not sought after and are often left on the table.

I will end this interlude with half a dozen recipes that I have tried. We can at any rate taste Bulgaria; a Bulgarian cookery book is now overdue.

TARATOR SOUP

Ingredients

Cucumbers	Wash the cucumbers, peel and dice.
Sour milk	Place in the sour milk that has been
Water	thinned and well stirred in cold water.
Walnuts	Spice with finely ground garlic, salt,
Vegetable cooking oil	dill and oil. Served cold, sprinkled
Dill	with ground walnuts.
Garlic	
Salt	

MONASTERY SOUP

Ingredients

Dry beans	Clean the beans and steep in water for
Carrots	from 8 to 10 hours. Place in cold water
Celeriac	add the oil and bring to the boil. Dice
Onions	the carrots, celeriac and onions, leaving
Tomatoes	the chillies whole. Add to the beans half
Parsley and mint	an hour before removing them from the
Vegetable oil	boil. Then add the tomatoes, mint, salt
Chillies	and black pepper.
Salt	
Black pepper	

SHOPPSKA SALAD

Ingredients

Peppers
Tomatoes
Cucumbers
Onions
Chillies
Vegetable oil
Vinegar
Salt
Parsley

Bake and skin the peppers and chillies and cut into fine strips. Dice the tomatoes and cucumbers, slice the onions and chop the parsley finely. Mix well and dress with oil, vinegar and salt.

MISH-MASH

Ingredients

Butter
Red Peppers (baked, peeled and seedless)
Tomatoes
Eggs
Parsley
Onions
Salt
Cheese
Chillies

Fry the onions in fat until soft. Cut peppers into small pieces, add to onions and fry for a few minutes. Peel the tomatoes, cut into pieces and add to the peppers. When the tomatoes are fried, mix eggs, cheese and chopped parsley and fry for a few more minutes.

PORK KEBAB

Ingredients

Pork
Lard
Leeks
Chillies
Red and green peppers
Tomato purée
Red wine
Salt
Black pepper
Paprika
Bay leaves

Bone and cut the meat into four or five pieces. Salt and add tomato purée, paprika, black pepper grains, bay leaves and wine. Bring to the boil over a slow fire till cooked. Add peppers, cut into small pieces and several whole chillies. Sprinkle with parsley before serving.

GUVECH

Ingredients

Lamb, veal
Beef or pork
Fat
Carrots and celeriac
Red peppers
Tomato purée
Parsley
Onions
Rice
Salt
Paprika
Black Pepper

Cut the meat, fry in hot fat, add the onions, diced carrots and celeriac. Then add the tomato purée, paprika, salt and black pepper and the red peppers and tomatoes cut into pieces. Pour stock over this and simmer. When the vegetables are cooked add the rice and boil for 15 minutes. Sprinkle with parsley.

The aroma of this last dish, a friend assured me, is the most likely to induce nostalgia in the Bulgarian abroad.

5. SOFIA

Fortified by a good meal we can now go sightseeing, selectively and always bearing in mind that people are more important than monuments, though, in this of all countries, the monuments mean more to the people themselves than to the visitors.

There are in Sofia some fifteen museums; in eleven of them few foreigners set foot. They are devoted to revolutionary and literary heroes; in Bulgaria poets and men of action go hand in hand, and are for the most part situated in the house where the man lived. Such biographical museums, when one is interested in the subject, have an extraordinary charm, bringing one more closely in touch with the personality than many chapters of biography.

There are two in other countries that are fixed in my mind in vivid detail, right down to the pince-nez and the pack of cigarettes on the desk; Tchekov's villa at Yalta – I have never seen a Tchekov play without the image of his books, pictures and furniture – and Puccini's lakeside home at Torre del Lago. I can imagine therefore what the Vazov or Vaptzarov home-museums must convey to the Bulgarian on such intimate terms with their work. From the tourist's point of view the most important museum, opened in 1965, is in the crypt of Alexander Nevsky, the most impressive building in the city. It dwarfs but does not detract from the beauty of the Church of St Sophia that gave its name to the city. This sixth-century church was converted into a mosque in the sixteenth century and then, shattered in an earthquake, fell into ruins. It has been superbly restored and occupies a very special place in the affection of the citizens. It has its place in a quartering of the city's coat of arms.

The Alexander Nevsky Memorial Church was built in 1912 as a tribute to the Russians who had died to liberate the country. It was designed by A. N. Pomerantzev, a professor of the Academy of Fine Arts at St Petersburg. It is that kind of building. It is impressive, however, by its sheer size, its splendid site and its white granite and marble surmounted by shining gold cupolas. From a distance, when the sun catches the domes, it has real beauty. The interior is large enough to support the many frescoes, the ikons and the elaborate ikonostasis, whose treatment varies from conventional neo-Byzantine to Brompton-oratorial. Mass is held there daily.

The museum in the crypt, an extension of the National Gallery of Art, shows more vividly than one could imagine the poverty of the religious art of the last fifty years. In any other country I would have written of the past one hundred and fifty years but in Bulgaria the second renaissance, still so recent, had all the vigour of a people forcibly cut off from civilisation and struggling to assert itself. Here in the vaulted crypt, against simple whitewashed walls and in a setting for which they were designed, one can see ikons from all parts of Bulgaria, dating over many centuries. One is amazed at their variety, from the naïve to the highly sophisticated, their humanity and the superb manner in which these artists could communicate to a devout and simple people. The rigid canons of the art did not then and should not now inhibit the true artist.

Housed there also was one of the greatest of all archaeological finds, the treasure of Panagurichté, usually exhibited in the archaeological museum at Plovdiv.

This treasure, found a few years ago by two brothers digging clay for brick making, consists of nine massive gold drinking vessels as elaborately decorated as the work of a Cellini. They evidently belonged to a Thracian nobleman of the eighth century B.C. They consist of *rhyta*, *oinochoae*, a phiale and an amphora, all in mint state, superbly decorated with scenes from Greek mythology, the Odyssey and the Iliad.

For the art-loving tourist this museum, the Boyana Church and the Rila monastery alone justify a visit to Bulgaria.

The National Gallery of Art, founded in 1948, in the former Royal Palace, is not rich by international standards. It is modern, but outside the main stream, stopping at early impressionism. For that very reason I found it all the more interesting for the light it throws on the Bulgaria of today. The more recent paintings and sculpture belong to the socialist-realist school and one might, from previous experience, expect the usual succession of set pieces from the life of Lenin, busts of Marx and Engels and massive carvings of impersonal field and factory workers. There are workers in plenty, but there are also nymphs and *baigneuses* and the French influence, previously so strong in south-east Europe, still persists. There is no great subtlety but humanity and humour are always present, even when the incidents depicted are heroic; it is difficult for the Bulgarian not to be lyrical. One never gets the impression, not infrequent in socialist art galleries, of being shouted at by loud-speakers. These lusty peasants can enjoy a joke even when exceeding a work norm or fulfilling a five-year plan. The stakhanovite descends from his pedestal. Motherhood – the peasant mother nurses her baby and not a nation – and the family are popular subjects. Ivan Milev's 'Rustic Madonna' (1925), Hristo Stanchev's 'In the Field' (1937) and Vassili Stoilov's 'Bulgarian Madonna' are particularly charming examples.

For the Bulgarians their most outstanding painter is Vladimir Dimitrov (1882–1960), always known as 'the Master'. It is easy to see why. A fine draughtsman and a magnificent colourist, he specialised in interpreting the Bulgarian people with a heroic simplicity that stressed the personality and vigour of a new nation with a future. This is patriotic painting, but never self-conscious, pompous or official.

The most interesting painting in this gallery is the self-portrait of Zahary Zograf whose work, so richly imaginative and bursting out of the narrow conventions of his day, can be seen at the Rila, Bachkovo, Troyan and Preobrajensky monasteries and indeed all over Bulgaria. He is one of the very rare artists not listed in Bénezit's great dictionary. This portrait of the artist in national costume, paint-brush in hand, looks at us with all the assurance of a man who could say, 'None of the Masters of Turkey, Mount Athos, Rumelia or Jerusalem are my equals,' and who could depict any local bigwig he did not like as burning in hellfire, as well as placing two aunts, who had disinherited him, among the fallen women!

The second Bulgarian renaissance followed several centuries behind the rest of Europe and as so much in Bulgaria that is recent and yet far distant – the country went from donkeys to trains in a generation – Zograf has become the subject of a legend, a revealing one that shows that in the nineteenth century Bulgaria was still living in the Middle Ages. It was told by a clever writer, Pavel Spassov, in a prose poem, which has in the past few years become known throughout the country, has entered into the national consciousness and enriched it. It is called 'The Sinful Love of Zahary Zograf', and here it is as my friend Donka told it me in front of Zahary's portrait.

'THE SINFUL LOVE OF ZAHARY ZOGRAF'

Zahary was born in 1810 in Samokov, near Sofia. This small city was known for its artisans in woodcarving and in gold, silver and iron work. The name Zograf means mural artist and his father who had studied in Vienna and his elder brother both travelled the country decorating churches. At the age of ten Zahary became their pupil.

In the next house there lived Kosto, a wealthy merchant with a very beautiful daughter, Hristiyania. The houses were separated by a wall but the door was always open and the children saw one another daily and soon became childhood sweethearts. Then Zahary, by now a proficient painter, went away for some time on many commissions. On his return he was shocked to find the door bricked up. He learnt that his father had died owing money to his neighbour and that there had been a bitter family quarrel. He was in despair.

There was a wild branching damson tree growing in the Zograf garden. Eager to rejoin his sweetheart, Zahary climbs it and looks down over the wall. Hristiyania has grown up. He sees a beauty with raven black hair and green eyes working in the garden. She hears him, looks up and then turns away. Mystified and more eager than ever Zahary waits till midnight and digs a hole under the wall. For three days he waits but she does not come near the wall. Then at last he sees the moon shining on a white nightgown and they are face to face.

'Don't, not now,' she whispers to him. 'I promise I'll wait for you.'

They say nothing, but stand looking at one another until the Rila mountains are lit by the rising sun.

The next day he leaves, determined to earn the money to repay the debt and so put an end to the quarrel. He is full of self-confidence.

Many years pass; his confidence has been justified. He is rich and famous, the best-known painter in Bulgaria. In all his paintings, as one can see, Hristiyania is his inspiration for the Madonna. He buys a superb white stallion, fills his saddle-bags with silver and gold and sets out for home. The very first thing that strikes

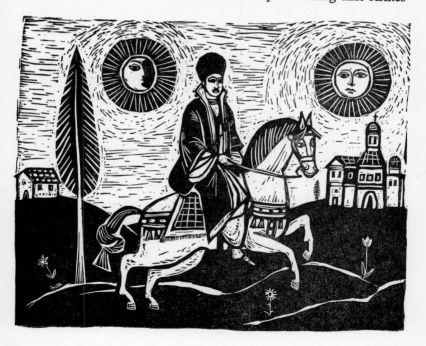

him is a door in the wall. So they have made the peace without him. He runs to the door of his house, he has the feeling that she knew he was coming and that she will be there, waiting. Promptly she greets him. 'Welcome home, *my brother-in-law*.'

He seeks an explanation; she is silent, her eyes downcast. He is desperately unhappy, tries hard to behave as if nothing had happened and in self-defence begins to boast of his great success with women. Still she remains silent. Finally his mother tells him that the Turks, noticing her great beauty, had begun to make advances to her and, receiving no encouragement, were threatening her father. He had held them off as long as possible but finally to protect her he had agreed that the only thing to do was for her to marry her neighbour in spite of the quarrel that had divided them.

Shortly after, Zahary marries a girl called Katerina, an attractive blonde with blue eyes. They have children, she is a devoted wife and mother but Zahary is still passionately in love with Hristiyania, at the same time hating her for what she has done to him. He is rarely at home now, his fame has grown still greater, beyond the boundaries of Bulgaria, and, supreme triumph, he has even been invited to decorate a church in Paris.

One night on returning home he finds her alone and asks her to walk with him in the garden. She feels his great distress and consents. He suggests that they elope. Indignantly she refuses; she will remain loyal to her husband and children.

'Never will I let them curse me, leave me you wretch, I never loved you. It was always a childish game.'

A flash of lightning reveals the anger in her eyes.

He leaves home that night; this time for years.

He is painting in Plovidiv when he hears of a terrible epidemic of the plague in Samokov. Anxiously he sets out and on the way meets a train of refugees, among them his wife and children and his brother. His brother tells him that Hristiyania had been given up for lost and that her last wish was for him to save the family; a man is needed on such a journey to protect them from the Turks. He hurries on to Samokov. The streets are deserted but for the howling curs. Everywhere there is the stench of death. There he finds her on her deathbed, alone. The best doctors have given up

all hope; there are others they might still save. He nurses her and then, for the first time, she speaks.

'I have always been in love with you and have pined for you. I would have kept my promise, in spite of all the risks, had I not heard that you were married to a Greek woman. When I learnt the truth it was too late. I was a dutiful wife. I loved my children.'

Having unburdened herself, she dies, but not before they had kissed for the first and last time.

Twenty days later Zahary was carried away by the same plague, but before he died he told his story in a delirium to Lavrentii, a monk from Rila, and it is from this that it has been handed down.

The tomb of Hristiyania can be seen in Samokov churchyard.

'Here lies our late mother Hristiyania, wife of Dimitri Zograf, and she lived forty-three years and was transferred to the eternal life in the year 1853, May 27th, the Holy Ascension of our Lord.'

History or fiction? Standing in Samokov churchyard I felt that surely it was true.

6. SOFIA

MUSEUM OF THE REVOLUTION

The next museum that I visited was situated in a long one-storeyed house with a stone courtyard surrounded by trees, formerly the residence of a politician. It looks cosy and harmless enough, yet many westerners, if they wandered in by mischance, would have felt themselves in mortal peril. It is the museum of the revolutionary movement.

There is such a museum in every communist city; all are informative and should be carefully studied, if one is to have the slightest notion of what is happening in the world today. One may then disapprove of the whole or disagree with some aspect of it, but one will at least learn what is common knowledge to every school-child and an intimate part of the pattern of thought of every adult in a large part of the civilised world. Also, we will come to realise that here the communists did not overthrow, with bloodshed and terror, a respectable and progressive democratic *bourgeoisie* such as our own but a system that was brutal, corrupt and, worst sin of all, historically completely out of date. In civil war there is bloodshed in plenty and much injustice, private feuds flourish, the innocent suffer with the guilty, but civil war is a temporary state. And when we step out into the street and observe the life of the people we can see that those men whom half the world regards as saints and the other as devils had ideals and a passionate sense of values. When the hating came to an end, they knew how to love. Such visits are reassuring to the unprejudiced with a sense of history. In the USSR or Bulgaria you cannot believe in another war; the accent is on construction, progress is proudly measured.

Today this seems to me such a truism that I hesitate to write it but I remember the tremendous impact that the first revolutionary museums I visited in Russia had on me when suddenly the bogy men were presented as martyrs and heroes. I did not and I do not always agree with their methods but I have learnt to respect their ideology. We have been conditioned from the nursery to identify romance and knight errantry with the aristocrat. We suffer from a Percy Blakeney-Pimpernel fixation that is often stronger than reason.* Dickens depicted both sides, but through this conditioning it is the mob and the guillotine that remain in the memory. Victor Hugo found a balance in *Ninety Three*; 'Let us state frankly that the Revolution committed crimes. Why conceal it? But we are of those who weigh the amount of evil mixed in with the good. The good predominates to an enormous extent. Even so it is necessary to maintain the highest principles.'

The museums of the revolution in Sofia and in other Bulgarian cities have a very special quality. A materialist philosophy has not discarded romance, which is now on the side of the people; revolutionary cells and partisan groups take the names of *haidouti* (heroes) and so many of these heroes are bards who translated Marxism into poetry. In Bulgaria too the blood was spilled by the Turks and fascists; the final revolution of September 1944 was so overwhelmingly popular that comparatively few were killed. The

---

* In the French Revolution some two thousand five hundred aristocrats perished. In the suppression of the Paris commune some twenty-five thousand workers.

greatest losses, over thirty-one thousand, were suffered by a united nation fighting against a common enemy, the Germans – a fact too little known in the West.

At the entrance to the museum the visitor puts on an outsize pair of felt slippers to protect the polished wooden floors and shuffles through the six exhibition rooms. We start with the bearded ones, the professors who look so much like a respectable group of Victorian worthies that photographs of Tennyson, Browning, Lord Salisbury and that supreme nobody, Mr Pooter who was Everyman, would not be out of place. Marx, Engels and, to us, a newcomer in Dimiter Blagoev, founder of the Bulgarian communist party, hang on the walls over showcases of their publications. They are followed by the men of action. There is the usual 'hand painted' picture of Lenin, walking along a canal in Petrograd; he was unfortunate in not having his David.

We now come to the activities of a very remarkable man, regarded by all as the father of his country, Bulgaria's George Washington.

GEORGI DIMITROV

I had already visited him in his mausoleum. There are no queues shuffling by; this is not a tourist attraction. I passed the wreaths, sheaves of official red-ribbon-bound flowers and simple posies and the motionless guards at the door, walked down a narrow dimly-lit corridor and came out into the chamber where Dimitrov lay in state. This is the portly, serene and jovial man so familiar from the busts and portraits of later years, the man who had achieved his greatest ambition of 'living to see communism established in Bulgaria'. In the museum we see him first in 1919 as a full-bearded intellectual, next the beard takes on a Lenin cut and then at Leipzig, clean shaven, there are photographs and sketches of him as he strides into world history dominating the courtroom.

There could be no doubt that this man was a giant. I knew something of his record but not enough. I wanted to feel the man himself and follow him through these many transformations. I went to the library and came back with a parcel of books. Alas, they were of little help. For the most part the documents and

speeches, which were of great historical interest, were wrapped
around in a pietistic jargon of sickly sentimentality. How wise was
Cromwell with his 'warts and all'. I read that he was fond of
children and had on one occasion sheltered some from the rain. His
and our greatest enemy had been known to pat children on the
head! Senators and MPs are baby kissers *ex officio*.

It is regrettable that the writing of communist history should
often be so poor. One expects the bias of a fixed philosophic view,
one expects the simplicity of style needed to appeal to the masses,
especially at a time when they were emerging from illiteracy. But
today these masses are among the best read and most cultured
people in the world and 'fascist beasts' and 'imperialist lackeys'
have worn thin as descriptive phrases, however effective they may
once have been as stump oratory. Let them take warning from the
Catholic Church; over-simplification and pietism are the greatest
causes of lapsed faith. Many of my Bulgarian friends as well as high
party officials both in Russia and Bulgaria agree that this phase of
vituperation is now an anachronism; fortunately so much of Bulgaria's revolutionary history, as we shall see in the very next room,
has been told by poets. Dimitrov still awaits his Botev or his
Vazov. I had to go direct to the transcripts of the Leipzig trial
for a glimpse of the real Dimitrov: brave, subtle, essentially
tolerant, well educated and always full of the earthy humour of his
country.

Dimitrov is as common a name as Smith or Jones and this also
is a way in which the people can identify themselves with him. He
was born in 1882. His father was a workman, his mother a farm-
hand and he was born in the harvest field. He was apprenticed as a
typesetter, a magnificent source of knowledge. At a very early age
he was influenced by Blagoev and especially by Tchernichevsky's
What is to be Done? This novel, written in a prison cell, inspired a
generation of revolutionaries. By the age of fifteen he had become
an active revolutionary, one who had the gall and daring to alter
and prune the articles of the reactionary Dr Vassil Radoslavov, the
man who had dragged Bulgaria on to the side of the Germans in
World War I. And Radoslavov remembered this when they were
both deputies.

'I've known you for a long time. Even when you were a lad you had the damned impudence to tamper with my articles.'

His story, so well recorded in the showcases, is that of all revolutionaries; meetings, speeches, pamphlets and hairbreadth escapes. Changes of name, appearance and passport. The highlight was a meeting with Lenin in 1921, when characteristically the supreme tactician told the inexperienced enthusiast, 'Don't let yourself be carried away.' This should have been remembered in 1923.

It was on September the twenty-third, 1933, that Dimitrov became a world figure when he spoke for the first time from the dock at Leipzig, charged together with another Bulgarian, Tanev, the German communist, Torgler, and the crazed Dutchman, van der Lubbe, with setting fire to the Reichstag. He spoke up boldly for his communist beliefs, for his life and, at that time, for the whole civilised world. The trial was a farce; Dimitrov had been kept in shackles for five months, which did not prevent him from making a profound study of German history. His defending counsel was a tool of the prosecution. Time and time again the presiding judge, the ridiculous Dr Bunger, shouted, 'Who is presiding here, you or I? Shut up.' Dimitrov did not shut up, there could be little doubt who was presiding.

Let us hear him in action at the moment when Goering takes the witness stand.

PRESIDENT (*to Dimitrov*) – I forbid you to make communist propaganda here.

DIMITROV – Herr Goering is making national socialist propaganda. (*Turning to Goering.*) This communist outlook on life prevails in the Soviet Union, the largest and best country in the world, and here in Germany it has millions of adherents among the best sons of the German people. Is this known . . .?

GOERING (*yelling loudly*) – I shall tell you what is known to the German people. The German people know that here you are behaving insolently, that you have come here to set fire to the Reichstag. But I am not here to allow you to question me like a judge and to reprimand me. In my eyes you are a scoundrel who should be hanged.

PRESIDENT – Dimitrov, I have already told you not to make

L'ACCUSE ACCUSATEUR

(Dessin de Boris Yefimoff.)

communist propaganda. That is why you should not be surprised if the witness is so agitated . . .

DIMITROV (*calmly*) – I am highly pleased with the reply of the prime minister.

PRESIDENT – Whether you are pleased or not is quite immaterial. Now I deprive you of the right to speak.

GOERING (*shouting at the top of his voice*) – Get out, you scoundrel. . . . Be careful, look out, I shall teach you to behave once you get out of this courtroom. Scoundrel!

Finally, a quote from Dimitrov's stirring peroration in which he invokes the saints!

> If the question of propaganda is raised, then may I fairly say that many utterances made within this court were of a propagandist character. The speeches here of Goebbels and Goering had an indirect propagandist effect favourable to communism, but no one can reproach them because their speeches have produced such a result.
>
> I have not only been roundly abused by the Press – something to which I am completely indifferent – but my Bulgarian people have also, through me, been characterised as savage and barbarous. I have been called a suspicious character from the Balkans and a wild Bulgarian.
>
> At the period of history when the German Emperor, Karl V, vowed that he would only talk German to his horses, at a time when the nobility and intellectual circles of Germany wrote only in Latin and were ashamed of their mother tongue, in 'barbarous' Bulgaria, the apostles Cyril and Methodius invented and spread the use of the old Bulgarian script.

After reading this I paid another visit to the man in the mausoleum.

We are back in the museum and the next rooms deal with the uprising of 1923 and the partisan movements of World War II.

THE UPRISING OF 1923

In June 1923 Alexander Stamboliiski, leader of the Agrarian Party and a strong opponent of the German alliance, the man who had rehabilitated postwar Bulgaria, was assassinated after a *coup d'état* and the notorious Tsankov seized power. The country was on the verge of civil war and extreme repressive measures were put into practice. The rule of law was suspended. The people, goaded beyond endurance, revolted under the leadership of Dimitrov and Kolarov, the moderate left joining with the communists.

The uprising of September 1923 was as abortive as that of 1876 and with thirty thousand dead, more costly. It ended in a complete fascist dictatorship and a drift from Moscow to Berlin. Like the previous revolt it was to be turned into victory, once again with the help of the Russians, but the period of waiting was longer – eighteen years instead of two.

We can best see it through the eyes of the poet George Milev, a non-communist, who wrote after the defeat:

> A hurricane has passed over our land such as neither we nor our fathers recall. It has shaken the deepest defiles in the Balkans and the remotest mountain valleys. The blood of brothers has spattered the grass and brushwood, the brain marrow of shattered skulls has stuck to the walls. The shrieks of men and the wailing of mothers strike high heaven. The winter fields are black with mourning scarves.

Milev was inspired by what he had seen. 'We intellectuals cannot, must not remain dispassionate to what the people experienced in September,' he wrote in the manifesto which introduced his new literary magazine *The Flame*. In it appeared his famous poem *September*. It was an act of extraordinary courage. It cost him his life, strangled by Tsankov's police, his body thrown into a ditch near Sofia. The publication was seized but the poem could not be stifled; one more poem that became a weapon.

In the room commemorating this revolt we can see the cudgels and pitchforks with which the peasants fought the well-armed police, manifestoes and photograph of the prisoners and the piles of dead bodies.

> Uprooted from villages
> Peasants are followed by troops
> In grim convoy
> To be shot.
> The order: 'Halt!'
> 'Prepare to fire!'
>   The bolts clatter:
>   Ku
>   Klux
>   Klan –
> 'Fire!'
>   – Bullets spatter.*

Thus Milev described the execution squads.

* Translation by Peter Tempest (Foreign Languages Press).

In the centre of the room there is a more powerful weapon, a field-gun of World War I. This was manned by the priest, Andrei, one of the heroes of the uprising, a true folk hero. Once again let Milev tell the story:

> There
> As dismay increased
> Alone
> Andrei
> The Priest
> To epic boldness
> Inspired
> Fired
> Round after round
> From the famous cannon –
> At last:
> With the shout of
> 'Death to Satan'
> In fury magnificent
> Turned about
> His cannon:
> Dispatched
> The final shot
> Straight
>   – at the House of God
> Where many a psalm he had rendered . . .
> And then he surrendered.
> 'Hang the Rev Priest on the spot!
> No cross, No grave! Let him rot!
>
> He was dragged to a telegraph pole,
> Close by stood the hangman
> And Captain
> The rope
> On the ground –
> Under the bitter
> Chill sky
> The Balkans
> Frowned.
> The priest stood full height,
> Massive figure of man,

All
Calm as granite –
No regret,
No remembrances –
Christ's cross on his chest
And eyes fixed on the crest
Of the distant hills,
On the future . . .
'Butchers!
'You lower your cowardly eyes
'In the hour a man dies!
'But – one death –
'What does it mean?
'Amen'
Tight lipped
He spat.
Then rapidly slipped
Himself
The noose on his neck
And
Not glancing heavenward
– Hung –
With teeth gripping
Tongue.
Majestic
Magnificent
Matchless!*

Thirty thousand dead, but in 1924, as we can see from photographs on the wall, thirty thousand others had the courage to attend the funeral of Dimiter Blagoev.

We pass through further rooms with their exhibits of faded pamphlets, clandestine printing presses, photographs of students and of poets, torches, home made weapons and forged papers. Every exhibit a story of courage and of the hope that 'The month of September shall turn into May'.

THE PARTISANS

Finally we come to the partisans of World War II, unlike their

* Translation by Peter Tempest (Foreign Languages Press).

5. The trial at Leipzig 1933. Georgi Dimitrov in the dock

6. Violetta Yakova (*right*) with friends

7. Pope André. A hero of the anti-fascist rising of 1923

8. Liliana Dimitrova in 1943

9. Liliana Dimitrova making a speech at the University, on the feast of St Clement of Ochrid. December 8, 1939

10. The outhouse at Marin Drinov St, Plovdiv, where Liliana Dimitrova fought with the police

11. Group at Kolibite, the Indian village at Varna

Front row : Donka Minkova and Vadim Rindin

Back row (left to right) : Mr Leisin, Mrs Haskell, Lili and Peter Dragoulieva and Galina Ulanova

12. Leisure at Varna, the author partnering Ulanova at an impromptu dance on a collective farm

Yugoslav brothers, unknown to us in the west. In this room there is the uniform of a gallant Major Thompson, an Englishman who came with the second brigade of partisans, formed in Yugoslavia to help the Bulgarians, and was tortured and killed. 'Why have you come here?' he was asked. 'I will die for liberty anywhere in the world,' was the answer. He is commemorated by the nameplate on a village railway station, Thompson, at the scene of his death near Sofia, and remembered by all.

Here also are the photographs of a number of young women, almost schoolgirls; Vela Peeva, *killed in action*, May the third, 1944, Violetta Yakova, aged nineteen, *tortured and killed*.

The snapshot of an adolescent taken at a carefree moment and torn, perhaps from some family album, tells us nothing. It was naïve to imagine that it would, but then in the past the tragic heroine has always come to us through the eyes of a painter. One looks at it repeatedly in amazement that anyone so frail and so essentially ordinary could of her own free choice become a commando. This was not someone to whom horrible things just happened in the course of war. Surely her expression must betray something of her quality? The very fact that it does not, that she is so very ordinary, is more moving than any work by a romantic or a so-called realist painter.

Violetta Yakova was born in 1923. Left an orphan at the age of eleven, she first went to work in a tobacco factory and later in a dressmaking atelier in Sofia. There she became an active revolutionary, trained as a saboteur and a fighter with all the thoroughness of a commando. One of her first outstanding acts was the total destruction by fire in September 1942 of a warehouse of furs destined for the German army's second winter in Russia. The damage was reckoned at several millions of *leva*. The following year she shot General Loukov, a former Minister of War, who was a particularly brutal fascist and a close Nazi collaborator. A price of three hundred thousand *levas* was now placed on her head. After other successful missions that included the killing of Colonel Pantev, a former chief of police, she took to the *maquis*, fighting with a number of detachments and for a time alongside the Yugoslav partisans. But in June 1944 she fell into a carefully laid police

D

trap in the village of Condofreille. Hiding behind the fountain in the village square she shot it out with the police, killing one and wounding two. She was captured and then cruelly tortured in an attempt to make her betray the organisation. In spite of this she managed to escape naked into the night. She could not get far and was shot and recaptured. Already half dead she was tortured once again with Nazi thoroughness, finally dying at Radomir hospital without having spoken a single word.

Inevitably there is the photo of a handsome young poet, Nikola Vaptsarov, tortured, sentenced and shot in 1942 and the manuscript of the last poem he wrote while awaiting execution:

> The fight is hard and pitiless
> The fight is epic, as they say:
> I fell. Another takes my place –
> Why single out a name!
>
> After the firing squad – the worms.
> Thus does the simple logic go.
> But in the storm we'll be with you
> My people, for we loved you so.*

There was one photograph that held my attention in particular, that of a young girl of striking beauty, black haired and with those matchless Bulgarian eyes. I was so moved by the picture, so very representative of all the young students I was meeting daily, that I returned to it many times and finally asked the curator for a copy.

Her name was Liliana Dimitrova; she met her lonely death at Plovdiv on June twenty-seventh, 1944, in a wooden garden shed, used for storing chicken food. I resolved to follow her short life from birth to its violent end and to find not merely the facts, as in the case of her colleague Violetta Yakova, but something of her personality. Her story should be widely known.

* Translation by Peter Tempest.

7. LILIANA DIMITROVA

My first day in Plovdiv I set out in search of Liliana.

On the crumbling stucco wall of a house at Number Five Drinova Street there is inset a bronze medallion on a marble surround, obviously designed from the photograph that I had. Under it is written with the same lack of inspiration:

> Here on June 27th, 1944
> Fell in the fight with the Fascist Beasts
> The nation's glorious national heroine
> Liliana Dimitrova (Blaga)
> Member of the Youth Organisation of the Central Committee
> Glory to the Heroine.

Some wreaths lay under the plaque; stiff and formal.

I pushed open the door and entered a shady courtyard that separated two houses. After a few moments an elderly woman came in with her shopping. On hearing what I wanted she called out to her neighbour, a young married woman, who invited me in and gave me a cup of tea, a glass of water and some strawberry jam, a traditional gesture of hospitality. Both women pressed me to stay.

'I remember it all so well,' my hostess told me. 'I was a school-girl at the time. I saw her lying dead. They put the body in a rough wooden coffin and bundled it on to a farm cart, driving away as rapidly as possible. People stood all around crying.'

I have a police photograph of her body, so horrible that I wish I had never seen it. Her youth and beauty are still recognisable but this is a thing on a slab and one can imagine the peering police taking photographs of the naked body from every angle, laughing and congratulating themselves at having laid so dangerous a criminal by the heels.

Liliana was born on July the twenty-seventh, 1918, in Constantinople. When she was three the family returned to Sofia. Her father, Nikola, had been a village schoolmaster for fifteen years. He was intelligent and well informed with a remarkable flair for understanding people. Kina, her mother, was firm and intelligent and an excellent housekeeper. She had the serenity and inner peace that is a special characteristic of Bulgarian women and that her daughter was to show even in the most adverse circumstances. Liliana may have inherited her political consciousness, her courage and resourcefulness from her paternal grandfather, commonly known as 'Dimiter, the bearded one', who played an active part in the movement to secure an independent Church and who was exiled by the Turks to the notorious Diabekir in Asia Minor.

Her education was the normal one, primary school and then Lycée Number Two for girls at Sofia. She studied what is called the semi-humanities course, Latin and modern languages. She had a passion for literature, her favourite reading being Cervantes, Byron, Molière, Schiller, Hugo, Tolstoy – especially *Anna Karenina* – and Zola's Rougon Macquart novels. She was stirred by Sienkewickz's *Sans Dogme*, Jack London's *Martin Eden* and *The Iron Heel* and Maxim Gorki.

She was also a great music lover. She once told a friend that she could never hear Schubert's 'Unfinished Symphony' without being moved to tears.

She finished her schooling in 1937 at the age of nineteen. She was clearly a sensitive and accomplished young person but never an introvert nor a prig. A friend of this period says, 'You might describe her as a really good, warm hearted girl. Very gay, so gay in fact that you could call her a *gamine*.'

In 1938 she went to the university. It was an election year, there was great excitement, especially among the young people and she had become an enthusiastic member of the General Union of Bulgarian Students (*Bons*), a left-wing organisation. One day when she was actively engaged in typing appeals there was a ring. Her brother, thinking it was a friend, opened the door. The police rushed in, seized the papers and arrested Liliana. It was her first encounter with the law. She was exiled for a short period to Omurtag in the Dobrouja.

Her return to Sofia coincided with World War II. The slogan of the left was 'Keep and Maintain our National Independence'. The masses remembered only too well the unnatural alliance with Germany; they loved Russia and feared another entanglement with Germany. The communists naturally looked to Moscow for leadership.

December the eighth, 1939, the feast of St Clement of Ochrid, was a university holiday. Liliana took part in organising a vast demonstration and made, as someone who heard it told me, a moving and splendidly reasoned speech outlining the role that science could play in a people's democracy. I have a snapshot of her making this speech, supported under the arms by two fellow students. She was by now an active communist.

The following year she went to work in a textile factory in Slatin. There her party work led to her second arrest. She was exiled once again, this time to Studenetz Razgrad.

On her return to Sofia she carried on with her underground work. Meetings were held in the sheltering forests of Vitosha. A friend remembers her at that time when every activity held greater dangers than exile. 'She was *svelte* and her chestnut hair was worn short. Her brown eyes were wreathed in an almost permanent smile. She was always gay. Liliana had a rare capacity for happiness.'

In 1941 Germany invaded the Soviet Union and once again a Bulgarian Government committed the country to an active pro-German policy. The young communists had to go into deep hiding, especially those with a record. The Nazis were working hand in hand with the police.

On the night of the second of July, Liliana made a good-bye visit to her home. It was being watched and she was surprised by the police. She managed to jump through a window, hurting her leg severely as she landed. Suffering intense pain, she dodged in and out of alleyways until she had finally shaken off her pursuers. She then went to a friend's house and rang the bell. People in those dark days, fearful of the police, did not willingly open their doors after dark and she was forced to spend the night in the street. When at daybreak the door was opened, she was taken in. By now her leg was considerably swollen and she was hidden and nursed for ten days.

She was very much a wanted person, and if caught, the Fascist police, fully under Nazi domination, would show her no mercy. She had become secretary of the Komsomol of the working district of Coniovitsa and a member of the Sofia regional committee.

One evening after a meeting Liliana and a group of young communists were stopped by the police who had cordoned off the district. They were asked for their papers. 'At once,' replied one of them, Marko Dobrev, and drawing a Mauser he shot a militiaman. As reinforcements came up they were caught in a hail of bullets. Liliana could hear them whistling past her. It was her first experience under fire and she found herself quite without fear. Once again she escaped, darting through the dark streets and alleyways she knew so well.

Her third arrest came totally unexpectedly and this time she was condemned to a concentration camp for women, St Nicholas in the Rhodope mountains. There she found two friends, Mara Petliakova and Yordanka Nikolova. Both were subsequently to be killed in partisan battles, Yordanka with the English Major Thompson. All well thinking people were on the same side in those bravely uncomplicated days. The three girls decided that with so much work to be done it was out of the question to remain prisoners. During dinner one evening they made a daring escape that involved a considerable feat of mountaineering. They lived wild in the woods for some time until finally they found their way to Plovdiv, where friends hid them.

In 1942 Liliana returned to Sofia where she became a member of the Central Committee of the Union of Young Workers. Now she was more active than ever, running risks at every moment. This time to fail meant a death sentence.

On May the twenty-fourth, feast of Cyril and Methodius, she organised a public anti-fascist meeting, relying for safety on the very boldness of the plan. The whole district was sealed off. Once again it was her fleetness and her knowledge of the city that allowed her to slip through and to find refuge in a friend's house where she hid bent double in a divan locker until, after four hours, the chase was called off.

It was at this time that she confided to a friend that she was deeply in love and unhappy. The man was a fellow worker and married. She had the strength of mind to keep silent though they were constantly thrown together.

Now she could never remain in one place for any length of time. Only the thick woods round Sofia provided a friendly refuge. 'One winter night, and how bitterly cold it was,' a fellow worker tells, 'we were exhausted, we had had nothing to eat for a long time.' 'We must keep warm, let's dance,' said Liliana. 'What shall we dance?' 'A waltz, of course.' And so they hummed and waltzed and kept warm. Later, when we meet him, we shall see that she was a true daughter of Levski, the lion.

On returning from the wilds her comrades, seeing that her dress was in shreds and her toes sticking out of her shoes, wanted to get her a new outfit. 'What I really need at this moment,' she told them, 'are some firearms and ammunition.' They gave her a Dreiser (calibre 7·65) and a Beuret (calibre 9).

'She shrank from killing,' a friend told me, 'she was extremely sensitive but she considered herself at war and she loved her country. There were two things about her, she never lost her sang-froid in a tight corner nor her sense of humour.'

Her narrow escapes were daily occurrences, but there were two that gave her particular satisfaction. The first took place during the period of massive allied air raids. The alarm had gone and the bombs were beginning to fall. Liliana who was hiding in an electricity supply factory jumped into an empty reservoir only to find herself in the company of two policemen. Then the reservoir began to fill and the men gallantly offered to take the heavy bag that was stopping her from getting out. It contained her armoury. 'No,' she told them laughingly, 'I've found a way, look,' and gripping the handle in her teeth, she let them lift her out by the arms.

By 1944 even the friendly Sofia had become too dangerous and she took the opportunity, caused by the confusion of the mass evacuation, to escape to Plovdiv. This city was in need of workers, the previous group having been wiped out, and Liliana became secretary of the local organisation and the inspiration of a group of saboteurs. She lived under the assumed name of Blaga in a one-storeyed, two-roomed house, 1 Ladjene Street, with a widow working woman and her son. It was here that the second escape that she so enjoyed describing took place.

The police rushed the house only just giving her the time – always on the alert she needed very little – to push open and clamber through a trapdoor into an attic full of untanned sheep-skins. The police, seeing the trapdoor, poked their heads in and hurriedly withdrew them. 'Phew, the stench is so awful,' she heard them say, 'nobody could possibly be hiding here.'

But now her time was running out. Her most important work was to reconstitute the movement of youth organisations in the different regions. She was working with a skilled and devoted band of young people; the police always close on their heels. One night in the street now named for her, the police tried to arrest them. A boy opened fire calling out to Liliana to follow him. As they ran, just ahead of their enemies, she lost her companion at the approach to a small church. This was not her friendly Sofia whose alleyways had saved her so many times. She darted in and out of streets and once again found a yard to conceal her. In it there was a small hut, sometimes used as a summer kitchen but now as a place for storing chicken food. For the moment she was safe, at any rate until daybreak. But then her luck deserted her. An air raid warden on his rounds heard a noise in the yard and suspecting something wrong informed the police.

They now came in a large company, finally a hundred of them. They started to fire. She fired back and they must surely have imagined that they had the whole group cornered. As the fight continued two of them were killed.

The battle between a girl and a hundred policemen lasted for eleven hours; a final shot and then silence. The police had failed; with that final shot, her last bullet, she had killed herself.

Her memorial is neither the bronze photograph nor the street name but a photograph that I so often saw hanging in the entrance to a school or kindergarten where at home there are the cups, shields and records of some distinguished former pupil. More fittingly even, at nightfall in one of the many pioneer camps that bear her name.

The pioneers stand in two lines, facing the flag. The eldest child reports to the camp leader,

'All present, except our immortal namesake, Liliana Dimitrova.'

8. OPERA, BALLET AND DRAMA

OPERA

Opera is a flourishing art in Bulgaria but by some extraordinary oversight it is kept a dark secret from the tourist. The result is that after a night in Sofia he rushes to sun himself on the coast and so loses any chance of meeting the Bulgarian other than in the anonymity of a bathing suit in which a collective farmer and a Texan millionaire look pretty much the same. There is no poster display or booking facility in the hotel lounge and the posters in the street are all written in Cyrillic that turns the too familiar *Faust* into *ΦΑΥCT* a mystery to most. Balkantourist, so skilled in producing well illustrated brochures, that are complete enough to serve as guidebooks, has not a single leaflet commending its opera.

The whole history of music in Bulgaria is a fascinating one and has much to teach us about the people as a whole; their ambition and the tremendous speed and thoroughness with which they set out to achieve it.

Before 1878 Bulgaria did not possess a single professional musician. There was a rich folk art and songs were used to express the moods of the people, their love of liberty and to celebrate the deeds of their heroes. Songs became deeds. The first formal music to be heard came from the military bands when, after the liberation, a

Bulgarian army was established. These bands played not only military marches but symphonic arrangements. This soon led to the establishment of orchestras. At the same time many choirs were set up in the cities. These beginnings were largely in the hands of Czech conductors who gradually formed the musicians. Here was the raw material for opera. At this time also, a number of Bulgarians who had been educated abroad returned, among them some singers and musicians. They organised an opera section of the newly formed national theatre and on January the second, 1891, there took place the first performance of opera in Bulgaria, a modest affair consisting of scenes from *Il Trovatore* and *The Merry Wives of Windsor*. The conductor and most of the singers were Czech. It was an exciting novelty but the new State had other things to occupy it, among them a number of wars and a change of dynasty. Sofia was still a large village or a very small town. The operatic section was soon dropped. It was not until 1908 that it was started once again, this time permanently, opening with a selection of scenes from *Faust* and *Il Trovatore*. The company consisted of a group of enthusiastic amateurs and half a dozen soloists; there was neither a regular chorus nor an orchestra. It was only in 1910 that it was possible to give a complete opera, Rubinstein's *Demon*. After that it grew rapidly, especially under the influence of Russian realist production, which had come about through the teaching of Stanislavsky. Many of its singers began to be heard on world stages. Soon also composers were beginning to write operas on national themes, and guest artists from abroad, among them Chaliapin, began to sing in Sofia. The village was now a capital city.

After the revolution the pace accelerated. The opera was given a home of its own, opera houses and companies were formed in the cities of Plovdiv, Roussé, Varna, Stara Zagora and Bourgas and operetta companies in the smaller towns.

This multiplication of companies makes the training of young singers and conductors an easy matter, gives composers increased opportunities and creates a healthy rivalry. It solves the problem that we have found so burdensome with Covent Garden and Sadler's Wells, both in London and no permanent company anywhere else. It is worth mentioning once again that the total population of Bulgaria is less than that of Greater London.

The Opera in Sofia is an ensemble opera in which the majority of the artists take both large and small roles. It has a repertory and not a *stagione* system. It consists of seventy soloists, a hundred and ten chorus, eighty dancers and two orchestras. There are six conductors and six producers. There are some thirty operas in the repertoire, with five or six new works produced every year. It is directly attached to the Council of Ministers. There is no rigid budget. It is provided with sufficient funds to fulfil its purpose.

The repertory is international: Italian, German, English, French and Bulgarian. All operas except the Russian are sung in Bulgarian. Every Bulgarian opera approved by the Union of Composers is bought by the State and put on the stage.

The repertory problem, even under such ideal conditions, is very much the same as in London, though the management has no need to look nervously at the box-office returns. The public likes the old familiar works and is shy of the new. *Peter Grimes*, for instance, was pronounced a 'jewel' by the critics, the singers and the specialists were enthusiastic, but once the period of curiosity is over it will not draw a Puccini house. The same thing occurs with national works. The critics are trained musicologists, and tend to be severe. As always they are disliked by the artists, who find them destructive. Critics see all casts before writing their articles. They have adequate space in the daily press and as much as they require in the cultural magazines.

I visited the opera a dozen times in a fortnight in Sofia and watched rehearsals in Plovdiv. Unfortunately I did not see a single Bulgarian work and only one opera new to me, Prokofiev's *Semyon Kotko*, an exciting music drama of events in a Russian village during the 1917 Revolution. Sofia specialises in *Boris Godounov*, there are five changes of cast, the bassos are outstanding and this year Karajan produced *Boris* for Salzburg with six Bulgarian singers. Boris Christoff, Nikolai Giaurov, Nikolai Gyuzelev, bassos, and Nikolai Nikolov and Dimiter Usunov, tenors, and Rayna Kabaivanska, soprano, have sung all over the world.

The tenors and sopranos are particularly at home in the *bel canto* of Italian opera. Katya Popova, beautiful and a moving actress, is considered in Paris the best Manon of the day. I have never heard or seen a more moving Tatiana.

A pleasing innovation is the summer dress of the orchestra, open-necked white shirts. This was very noticeable and my only criticism of the Sofia Opera House was that the orchestra is raised too high and on occasions tends to drown the singing, especially from the grand tier. I am told that the reason for this was that the orchestra was bored at being so low down in the pit. True or not, I can sympathise.

On the steps of the Opera House there stands a gigantic statue of the assassinated agrarian leader Stamboliiski, hand in pocket as at the moment of his death. It is completely out of proportion to its surroundings but, like the Albert Memorial, it is looked upon with affection. The people say that, however booked up the performance, Stamboliiski always has a ticket.

THE VARNA BALLET CONTEST

The Bulgarians believe that one of the functions of a small country is to encourage international cooperation in the arts and this they do on a very large scale with chamber music contests at Plovdiv, operatic singing at Sofia* and ballet at Varna.† On these occasions east and west meet on the most relaxed terms and artists and intellectuals get to know an aspect of Bulgaria hidden from the tourist. The resulting friendships have been maintained; our Alan Rawsthorne and Bryan Balkwill are known and appreciated by countless people whom I met. In the operatic contest two English singers won gold medals, Peter Glossop and Ava June. Both have revisited the country as guest artists. England is respected through its musicians. It is only when one travels that one comes to realise the great work done by the British Council, operating, alas, on a shoestring – a very short-sighted policy.

The ballet contest, my original reason for visiting Bulgaria, has proved exceedingly interesting for dancers, judges and public alike.

* In 1963 one hundred and one competitors from twenty-seven countries took part.

† In 1965, seventy competitors from fourteen countries took part.

It is held for dancers under the age of thirty. In the first round they have to dance an excerpt from the classics, for the second and third rounds, if they are successful in passing, they may present a work of their choice.

The judges under the chairmanship of Galina Ulanova are drawn from some fifteen countries; they have included Serge Lifar, Erik Bruhn, Geneviève Guillot, head of the ballet school of the Paris Opera, Frederick Franklin, director of the Washington ballet, such great Soviet personalities as Theodore Lopuhov, Tatiana Veceslova, Elena Cherkassova, Luciana Novara, from La Scala, Milan, and ballet masters from Czechoslovakia, Yugoslavia, Cuba, Germany (East and West), Holland, Hungary, Rumania and the host country. Dancers have come from as far afield as Japan.

It is a warming sight to see the legendary Ulanova as the chairman of a committee. When I told her that she was a legend in London she remarked that it must be because she had danced so few performances. She is humble – modest is not the right word – and reserved, easy to admire and very difficult to know. My close association with her in Varna has, after an acquaintance of nine years in London and Moscow, made her into a friend. The education she has given me from watching her dance, seeing her teach and listening to her judgement has, after half a century's experience, altered my whole conception of the possibilities inherent in dancing. Her personality is obviously immense but she never tries to dominate. As a teacher she studiously avoids imposing her interpretation on the pupil but guides him to develop his own personality and to get the most from his physique and temperament. I disagreed with her once on what seemed to me a too lenient view of an interpretation of Giselle. 'I must know best,' I told her, 'I have more experience. You never saw Ulanova dance it.' She was astonished. 'Do you honestly think I was as good as all that?' As the chairman of a polyglot committee of vastly differing experience she remains an artist. She feels strongly but she never raises her voice, she lets everyone speak, and some do off the point and at considerable length, she sums up at regular intervals and finally the solution is found. She goes on every excursion and attends every banquet, getting to know all her colleagues and forming shrewd, firm but charitable judgements. The effort must be tremendous in so retiring a person, the least theatrical of the very many artists I have known.

I have already mentioned the role of the translators who make such occasions possible. The Concert Direction who organises these events runs into the usual difficulties, laughs heartily and solves them.

The lesson of the Varna contest is unique in the history of ballet, and not surprisingly so. Here is the opportunity to see on one night some dozen interpretations of a familiar work by dancers of different nationalities, experience and school. It is a lesson in national temperaments as well as in the dance. It proves, among other things, the extraordinary richness of the classical dance, the dance created to reveal the dancer's full potential. Given the essential technique there are many ways of attacking any dance, each one valid. Yet the great dancer is instantly recognised by the jury, in spite of its different viewpoints, so is the bad dancer. It is in the adequate performance that the differences of opinion arise and here the discussions are most revealing. The reaction of a public not yet very familiar with ballet is also interesting. During the first round anything that seems at all difficult is applauded then, as the contest proceeds, the applause becomes more discriminating, until finally experts and tyros seem to be of one mind. It is in the classic round that quality is revealed, later when the dancers perform works specially created for them, they rarely fail to make an impression.

The classics not only compete with our memory of great occasions, they need 'filling in', especially under the existing conditions. The open-air theatre is of great beauty, with its vine-covered walls, fringed by trees and the star flecked blue of the sky above, but Giselle has no grave, the *wilis* and their baleful queen are absent, piano replaces orchestra and the dancer is faced with the challenge of providing the whole context. It is here that one saw the tremendous gulf that separates the inexperienced from the true professional. Often the talented student at the beginning of a career could call upon a greater technique but the professional at his best, quite apart from stagecraft, is creative. He does not dance steps but something that is a dramatic whole and when there is more than one dancer they play to one another. Two years on the stage make all the difference. For this reason it has been decided for the future to have both a student and a professional class.

Already Varna in its two years has seen some remarkable performances; notably by Vladimir Vassiliev, today in a class of his own, and Ekaterina Maximova. Just how good they were one could judge from the *Don Quixote pas de deux*, danced after we had seen it performed some twenty times and could barely tolerate the dated music any longer. We hummed it, dreamed of it, dreaded it. But now it was no longer a bravura piece, a technical endurance test, *ham* in excelsis, but something of extraordinary elegance. It was so easy and unforced, so light and witty, so very real that one felt that one had misjudged Minkus and that he was a composer after all. Now we were seeing it for the first time. I realised that I had waited over thirty years, since Pavlova's time, to enjoy this work again.

It may be asked whether an international competition on such a scale is needed to tell one that Vassiliev and Maximova, Sizova, Makarova, Tikhonov, Lavrovsky and Besmertnova are great dancers. Certainly not, but they set the high standard against which true discoveries can be made and in two years many discoveries have been made; the Bulgarians, Vera Kirova and Krassimira Koldamova, the Russian Malika Sabirova, since admired in England and especially these amazing Cubans, Loipa Araujo, Josefina Mendes and Aurora Bosch, long limbed, stylised, exotic and magnificently feminine. At Varna two years running it was shown that Cuba, under the guidance of that magnificent ballerina, Alicia Alonso and her husband, Fernando, had become a great power in ballet.

Varna also showed that male dancing is coming into its own again and that there are boys from Hungary and Poland, Finland and Japan now in the great tradition. The men impressed us more than the women.

What of the well-established ballet countries, England, France, Denmark and the United States?

Their difficulties are many and, alas, stand out. They have been underlined in the Soviet Press and there is little one can answer. The socialist countries find it worth while to give their dancers leave, to finance them and send them in as a team while the capitalist nations have no funds for such a purpose. The Bulgarians pay all the expenses in their country and generously, but the fares there and back must be found. So far only isolated dancers from the west have entered and they have been ambitious, courageous but very far from representative. It seems an opportunity missed, not to win medals, but to meet one's fellow workers, to exchange information and to make friends. I realised this aspect of Varna when the West German judge, in a toast, said that, for her, the greatest pleasure of all had been to meet her East German colleague in such surroundings. Varna is more than a contest, it is a top level conference in the field where such a thing is genuinely helpful. Such has been Bulgaria's intention in sponsoring these music and dance competitions.

Dancing comes as naturally as singing to the Bulgarians. I often saw them break off a modern dance in the ballroom, circle and join hands for the *horo*, a characteristic folk-dance, which I saw danced in farms and at village celebrations. It is taught to the pioneers and will never die, any more than Scottish dancing. It will inevitably undergo a change, complex steps and local variations will tend to drop out. It is closely bound up with peasant dress, which is now only worn on special festive occasions and the few times that I saw it it was worn with high heels and other of the refinements of urban civilisation. All the peoples' republics have been eager to preserve these dances and have done so with great skill, originating what has become a new form of entertainment. We have seen a number of these groups in London. The Bulgarians have a splendid folk ensemble where trained dancers and singers, but not professionals in the balletic sense, perform dances and sing ballads that have been collected in the countryside, a living folk museum. The dances have been arranged for the stage but not distorted or tamed. Apart from their intrinsic value they are invaluable as a source of choreographic material.

I saw but little of Bulgarian ballet, apart from a number of its dancers. It is of very recent growth. Its dancers are attractive, excel in the expression of a dramatic or passionate situation but still lack the meticulous classical training, the product of a great tradition. Two of its ballerinas seemed to me outstanding, Vera Kirova, who was awarded a gold medal and Krassimira Kolda-mova, a silver medallist. Its dancers are sent to Russia on scholar-ships but a better investment would be for Russian teachers to be in from the start rather than when the dancer is already a soloist and has developed faults that can no longer be remedied.

Varna revealed much lamentable choreography, as might be imagined. Many tried hard to be contemporary and landed themselves in the 1930's. They had not, like the Russians, a vast experience to draw upon, one that safeguarded them even at their least inspired, neither had they the dancers that could transform the commonplace into something exciting. There was a choreographic prize to be awarded but the jury was unanimous in deciding that this could not be done. Professor Theodore Lopukhov, with his vast experience, told us that he had spent a lifetime studying choreography as an art and that it was still impossible to formulate an objective standard. One could agree about dancers but not about ballets. It was thought that this might be a good subject for discussion the following year when for a couple of days the jury might become a conference.

To me the major difficulty in judgement and discussion is that unlike the musicians and dramatists we are still very ignorant of one another's work. The Englishman takes Ashton as a yardstick, the American Balanchine, the Russian Lavrovsky or Grigorovitch and there is no longer an international standard as was once set by a Fokine. There was one choreographer of great talent, a Bulgarian Bogdan Kovachev, who has, as a result of being seen at Varna, put on some ballets in Italy with great success. His *Daphnis and Chloe* is a considerable achievement.

DRAMA

The Bulgarian theatre in the hands of schoolmasters and gifted amateurs was a powerful means of awakening the national con-sciousness, during the long dark night of the Turkish occupation.

One of the liveliest chapters in Vazov's masterpiece, *Under the Yoke*, not surprisingly depicts such a scene; as we shall see, all Bulgaria lies between the covers of this book.

The Turkish bey has been invited to an amateur performance of an innocuous comedy. The chapter starts with a belly laugh and then . . .

The play ended with a song which the Count and the Countess, and their retinue took up: 'Count Siegfried now rejoice.'

But after the first two verses of this virtuously joyful song, the strains of a revolutionary song rang out on the stage:

> Blaze up in us, oh love so bright,
> Against the Turks we'll go and fight.

It was as if a thunderbolt had struck the hall. At first only one sang it, then the song was taken up by a few of the actors on the stage, then by all of them, and at last the audience itself took up the burden. A wave of patriotic fervour laid hold of everyone. The manly tune of this song grew like an invisible wave, filled the hall, flowed over into the yard and burst out into the night. . . . The song rent the air, stirred up and exhilarated people's hearts. These martial notes struck a new chord in the audience. Everyone who knew the song began to sing it, both men and women; it united all souls, made the stage merge with the hall and rose heavenward like a prayer. . . .

'Sing on, boys, long life to you!' shouted Micho ecstatically. But others among the older people protested under their breath, considering this mad rapture ill-placed.

The bey also listened with satisfaction to the song, of which he understood not a word . . .

Surely a vital beginning to a national people's National Theatre. Before the war there was a State Theatre in Sofia together with municipal theatres in Plovdiv, Bourgas, Varna and Roussé. There were in all thirteen dramatic companies. Today, there are forty-six State theatres and a dramatic academy, with an expenditure thirty times more than in 1939. The theatre plays to an audience of some seven million, out of a total population of eight million. In the last twenty years, in addition to the international classic repertoire, six hundred plays by two hundred and eighty contemporary

Bulgarian authors have been produced and three hundred Soviet plays.

Sofia is cut off from the live theatre of the west purely for economic reasons, only the French, so culturally mature, have thought it worthwhile to send a number of important productions from their national theatres. There is, however, a flow of visiting companies, in the past year from France, Russia, Poland, Greece, Yugoslavia and East Germany. The English theatre seen only in translation lags behind. The popular modern works are by Wilde, Priestley and Maugham and, from America, Steinbeck. *Of Mice and Men* has had a long run and a more recent play, William Gibson's *Two for the Seesaw*. One of the most significant ventures is the Satire Theatre, very outspoken and exceedingly popular with the young. It was created in 1957 as a cabaret in the Parisian manner to deflate the cult of personality but it soon became a theatre of ideas, produced non-realistically. Mayakovsky's *Bed Bug*, the first dramatic production, set the tone.

I have, and shall, avoid statistics that can be found in every yearbook, but those I have quoted are impressive and set an example to be followed. Where are the Manchester, Birmingham, Bristol, and Glasgow Opera Houses? How often do we hear of the failure of repertory companies in cities with a larger population than Sofia itself? How many cities in the United States lack their own professional company?

In 1964, the Shakespeare celebration year, the small city of Vidin (population twenty-nine thousand) gave a magnificent Shakespearian season, the setting a massive twelfth-century castle overlooking the Danube and this year it was followed up by a season of historical drama. The theatre was packed, not with tourists but by the proud and enthusiastic Bulgarians; not the least proud and enthusiastic were the local people. I have yet to hear anyone from Edinburgh or Bath ever characterise their Festival as anything but an amenity-disturbing nuisance (I have, of course, bowdlerised the customary words). Theatre tickets are cheap enough to be within the reach of most people and the Ministry of Culture and municipal officials think the very high budget well worth while. In fact it spends more per head on the arts than any other country.

I could only profitably sample the Sofia National Theatre, rightly named after Vazov, by a play I knew by heart, *The Seagull*. It was magnificently acted with a Moscow Arts Theatre feeling for teamwork and detail but it was not a Stanislavsky carbon copy. The production was imaginative and brought out aspects of the play I had never seen before. It even entranced my Russian wife!

9. IN KOPRIVSHTITSA

IVAN VAZOV

It is impossible to know the Bulgarians without having visited Koprivshtitsa, preferably after a reading of Ivan Vazov's *Under the Yoke*.

Vazov is Bulgaria's greatest and most prolific writer; novelist, poet and playwright. There are Vazov streets, Vazov museums, Vazov monuments and there is a Vazograd. He has made history live and he has created history. He is Bulgaria's Homer and Tolstoy; as always here, time is compressed.

Under the Yoke was written in Russia where Vazov had gone as a refugee in 1886, after the *coup d'état* which saw the removal of the then Prince of Bulgaria, Alexander of Battenberg. 'To fill up my time and deaden the *ennui* of an idle life, I thought of writing my novel, *Under the Yoke*.' It tells of the life of the Bulgarian people on the eve of liberation. It is based on personal observation and most of its characters are people he had known.

It is an epic novel by any standards; exciting narrative, sensitive characterisation and an irony and a play of light and shade too seldom seen in such patriotic works. Vazov realised that to be truly heroic is rare, that the majority of the people, unless driven to desperation, seek security. 'He hides from those he fears, he does not fawn,' wrote an English observer of the Bulgarian in Turkish days. He painted an unforgettable picture of the active collaborator, the *chorbadji*, one that was so often repeated in the Great War. His heroes are fallible; they have in them something of d'Artagnan and of Tartarin. He showed all his native tolerance with no hatred of the Turk in his right place, at home. His great dramatic scenes, intensified by his humour and humanity, are never set pieces. This is a book to be put on a shelf alongside *War and Peace*, *La Chartreuse de Parme* and *I Promessi Sposi*.

KOPRIVSHTITSA TODAY

Today Koprivshtitsa is a small town of great and serene beauty, both in its architecture and setting. Rivulets from the Sredna Gora mountains, spanned by graceful low arched bridges, cut it into segments, there are fountains of well-carved stone in every district. It is the highest town in the country and the only settlement in the Sredna Gora mountains not to have been burnt by the Turks.

The day I was there, busloads of schoolchildren had arrived on an outing and they were crowding round the mausoleum where the heroes of 1876 are buried, spelling out the words, 'Let us keep the national liberty for which the heroes of the rising of 1876 fell.' For them it was both picnic and history lesson. Seated on a bench was a very old and wrinkled man. I asked his age. 'I'm ninety-two,' he told my translator, 'give him my greetings.' At the time of the uprising of which the children were learning, he was nine years old. Perhaps he could remember some of the episodes that had made his town glorious, even though he might have forgotten what happened last week. I left him in peace, puffing his pipe and basking in the sun, but it made a vivid impression. I walked over the little bridge where the first shot had been fired and up to the Church of the Assumption built in 1817, buried half-way in the ground to keep within the height limits imposed by the Turks. In the graveyard there was an old woman in black, bent double with age, muttering to herself as she laid out her washing to dry on a tombstone. She was going through the motions laboriously but she was very far away and it was impossible to recall her. She too would have been alive then.

In that same churchyard I was attracted by the moving statue by Ivan Lazarov of a seated woman, watching and waiting. It was the tomb of the young poet Debelianov, killed in action in Greece in 1917. It celebrated his best loved poem: 'And in humble meditation she waits for the return of her child.' The country children were climbing all over the statue, a small girl standing on its head, a little boy nestling in the mother's lap. Up the narrow street, shaded from the hot midday sun, were the houses of the once prosperous citizens, rebuilt for the last time towards the middle of last century after having been burned and plundered for generations. The town is a museum; every house is a museum.

The wealthy merchants had vied with one another to provide the beauty, comfort and spaciousness they had seen in Vienna, Paris and elsewhere – *alafranga* (*à la française*) – was the word to describe dress and furniture, combining the best in Bulgarian wood carving with a kind of baroque that had been well adapted to the locality. There were broad verandas with comfortable couches, long low tables for coffee, window seats and small nooks for quiet retreat, where the householder could see without being seen. The houses were shut off from the cobbled streets by high walls with overhanging tiles and one entered through a wooden gate, studded with wrought-iron nails, stout enough to resist a battering while the owner, ever on the alert, hopped out by a back way into the woodland beyond, and from the woods into the dense forest. There were spacious courtyards sheltered by trees, each with a well, surrounded by flowering shrubs.

Today, Koprivshtitsa has the appearance of a village. It is a place of pilgrimage and not yet a noisy juke-boxed centre of tourism. In its heyday it was prosperous and busy with over twelve thousand inhabitants.

The Bulgarians founded many of their towns in the least accessible spots, hidden by the thick virgin forests, home of the wolf, the stag and the wild boar but kind to the man with a price on his head.

Exactly when it was founded is not known, but it soon flourished and became an important centre for cattle breeding and grazing and, later on, for the fur and woollen cloth trades. The Turks were in need of its products and the inhabitants, without giving up their independence of spirit, profited by this. Some of them even opened offices in Constantinople and succeeded in gaining special privileges, the most valuable of which was the right to winter their flocks in the sunny pastures of Thrace, an imperial preserve. They grew rich, learnt to read and write and added to their knowledge by travel. Abroad, they found out that it was possible for people to live without fearing the knock on the door, and this knowledge fostered their love of freedom. Koprivshtitsa became a centre of education, culture and revolution. The little pharmacy where the Koprivshitsa conspirators gathered meets one as one enters the town.

THE CHERRY-TREE CANNON

When one visits the town with its spacious, well furnished houses it speaks of anything but revolution; serenity, ease, wealth with perfect taste and education. Enter the elegant house of Todor Kableshkov and immediately history comes to life. The walls are covered with photographs and on the half landing there are two special exhibits, a cannon and a silk banner with a lion rampant. The cannon is like no other, it has never seen the inside of an ordnance factory. It is roughly carved out of a cherry-tree log and it looks like a cherry-tree log on wheels. Its ammunition consists of iron, bullets, gypsy nails and horseshoes. It has one advantage, that of great mobility, it can be carried on a strong man's back. There were twenty such guns.

'The insurgents,' writes Vazov, 'were burning with impatience to hear the voice of the first Bulgarian cannon. They were all as joyful and enthusiastic as children – some even wept.'

'Just listen boys, and hear the Balkan lion roar. His voice will shake the sultan's throne and tell the whole world that Stara Planina is free' ...
The gunner was setting to work.

'Wait a minute . . . we mustn't frighten the women and children, we must let them know first . . .'

A man with a strong voice warns the town that this is only a rehearsal and that they must not be alarmed.

'After the families had been warned the work was put in hand. Belcho struck fire, lighted a piece of tinder, stuck it on a long stick and placed it near the breech. The tinder caught fire and small clouds of blue smoke rose in the air. In feverish expectation of the report the insurgents ran off quite a distance, others lay down in the trenches, so as not to see anything, some even stopped their ears with their fingers and closed their eyes. Several minutes passed. The strain was terrible, it beggared description. The blue smoke still rose above the fuse without managing to set fire to it. Hearts beat as though they would burst. The suspense was becoming unbearable. Finally a white flame ran along the fuse which began to smoke too and immediately the cannon emitted a helpless, angry, rasping sound, as of a dry board being split, something like a sharp cough, and vanished behind a thick cloud of smoke. But the cough had torn the cannon open, and the charge was spat out only a few feet away. Many of the rebels who had taken cover did not even hear the explosion.'

The remaining cannons were hastily improved, bound with hoops and ropes and even lined with tin. In any case they were only meant to be fired once and that once in a fixed direction.

It is with guns such as these that the rebels were to challenge the Ottoman army. One of them is optimistically engraved 'End of the Turkish Empire. 1876'.

GEORGI RAKOVSKI

This is not a history. Deliberately I am only concerned here with certain highlights in the story of those personalities who came so very much alive to me that day and on the spot, men as remarkable as Garibaldi or Kossuth, but little known outside Bulgaria. Their ideals and acts influenced their country and continue to do so, and without them Bulgaria is not revealed. I have omitted many heroic names and also any study of the economic background of the time. This is a romantic point of view, in one sense a superficial one, yet it is the romance that has kept the names so intensely alive.

The story of revolt begins with the very first day of oppression and lasts all of its five hundred years. But revolt is hopeless and the brave men who attempt it are Robin Hoods, leading a vendetta rather than a planned national revolutionary movement. The monk Païssi begins the process of education, the Turks are weakening and there is now a strong potential ally in the Russians. The time has come for a fighting statesman with a clear vision and a technique of revolution. Georgi Sava Rakovski was the first of the moderns, though from the moment of his birth his story is a romantic one.

In 1821 there was a Russo–Turkish War and an uprising in Serbia. This brought hope to the Bulgarians and inspired the Turks to a still more brutal oppression. A band of Turks had come to despoil the village of Kotel. One man set out to parley with the Turkish leader, telling him that, if he spared the village, they would get all they needed; gold, cattle and leather. The Turk accepted and made him an administrative chief, the people thanked him and at the same time congratulated him on the birth of his son, Georgi.

The boy's mother – and this mother theme recurs in every one of these sagas where mother and mother country are so closely identified – was a sensitive woman who brought up her child on the songs and folk tales of the countryside. He studied in the village and then in Plovdiv, Constantinople and Athens. There he began to understand what it meant to be a Bulgarian, realising that as the first step to freedom the Church must become autonomous. He organised a group to read prayers in the vernacular.

In 1841 he went to Braïla in Rumania and started a school where he taught Greek, French and Turkish. A revolutionary band had just been wiped out and Rakovski planned a new and better organised guerrilla troop with himself as leader. At the last moment he was betrayed. The police surrounded the house but Rakovski, after killing two of them, managed to escape. For a time he found shelter with a Bulgarian family, only to be denounced again, tried and sentenced to death. He had gone to Rumania as a Greek citizen and it was therefore decided to take him in custody to Athens. However in Istanbul he was greeted by the Greek ambassador as a distïnguished guest. His father had been able to fix things. The next day under a changed name and disguised as a sailor he left for Paris where for a year and a half he studied at the Sorbonne. Finally, he returned to Kotel under yet another name. There he found that the wealthy *chorbadjis* had taken the upper hand and that both he and his father were suspect. Impetuously he upbraided them, and he and his father were arrested on suspicion and for half a year moved from prison to prison without a trial. When they were tried there was no proof. They were ransomed, put to prison once again, for over three years this time, and once again ransomed. Corruption and cruelty went hand in hand.

By now Rakovski knew the law very well and established himself in Istanbul as a lawyer and merchant. He soon made a fortune. His business took him all over Bulgaria but he never lost sight of his great objective. With the outbreak of the Crimean War, when paradoxically Tsarist Russia became the hope of the oppressed, he offered himself as a translator of Russian at the Turkish headquarters, a thirteen-year-old, Raicho Nikolov, swimming the Danube to carry the information to the Russians. Rakovski was discovered and, after killing his guard, fled to the Balkans with a small band to await the Russians. They had, however, been thrown back to the Rumanian bank of the Danube, the 'army' was disbanded and once again he returned in hiding to his native Kotel. There he studied folk-lore and began his famous poem *The Forest Traveller* (*Gorski Putnik*) for, of course, being a Bulgarian he is also a poet. The familiar pattern of escape, recapture and escape was repeated in Bulgaria, Serbia and Rumania. In 1858 he found himself in Odessa, home of all Bulgarian political refugees. There he studied Sanskrit and evolved a theory, since proved wrong, that originally the Bulgarians had come from India. He tried to edit a paper but the authorities found it inopportune and he was off again on his wanderings, once more to Belgrade where the ruling prince, Milos, an old friend was able to protect him. There he began his paper, *The Swan of the Danube*, advocating Church separatism as the first step to political independence. The paper soon became a rallying point for patriotic Bulgarians who now thought of him as 'our Garibaldi'.

In 1861 his aim was a double one, to educate the Bulgarians and to inform the outside world. He evolved a new plan, to organise *legia* of about one thousand armed men, first to free Serbia and then to march with the Serbian army and liberate his own country. The Serbian authorities approved the plan. The rebel became an unofficial ambassador. He corresponded with European ministers, rallied the *haidouti*, drilled his troops and wrote manifestoes. For a time he played an active role in the fighting between Serbians and Turks but as the international situation grew more and more complicated the great powers intervened.

The early figure of Rakovski, the fighter-conspirator, lean, with a long thin moustache, might have passed for a close relation of Robert Louis Stevenson. Now in his mid-forties he was in the prime of life and looked it; a fine figure of a man with mutton-chop whiskers and something of a dandy. One of his secretaries, thought he suffered from megalomania. It was not true; he had a part to play and must keep up appearances as he visited capital after capital, trying to organise a Balkan Union. All agreed, each wished to be the boss. In 1863 he stayed in Athens for two months. It was the happiest, indeed the only peaceful interlude in his life.

He had fallen in love with Phroso, daughter of a wealthy merchant. They walked in the Acropolis by moonlight and became engaged. But once on his travels again he realised that he could not allow himself to be distracted. 'I love you,' he wrote, 'but now I must fight for the liberty of my people.'

The following year he was taken ill with consumption and spent several months in a monastery. The revolutionary committee was almost disintegrating and a former secretary declared himself the leader. When Rakovski met him, he, Rakovski, was made to take an oath to be true to Bulgaria.

He died in 1867, near Bucharest, within eleven years of the promised land.

VASSIL LEVSKI

The most attractive, the best loved and the most farsighted of all the revolutionary leaders was Vassil Levski, who, directly inspired by Rakovski, took his place in the struggle for emancipation.

Vassil Ivan Kounchev – Levski meant lion, the symbol of Bulgaria – was born in Karlovo in the Valley of Roses on July the sixth, 1837. He was seventeen years old when his father died and was put in the charge of his uncle, a wealthy monk in the monastery of Hilendar, birthplace of Paissi's great history. When his uncle moved to Stara Zagora, Vassil accompanied him. He proved an excellent student and, tempted by his uncle's promise to send him to study in Russia, he became a monk. His uncle did not keep his promise.

Vassil cast aside his habit and joined Rakovski's volunteer legion, later entering the military school in Belgrade. There is a picture of him at this time; a young dandy in frogged and braided uniform with carefully curled moustachioes. He clasps his sword, standing by a pillar on which rests his plumed shako. For the first and last time in the Balkans I was looking at Ruritania, this surely is the portrait of Rupert of Hentzau! Vazov describes him as of medium height and *svelte*, with grey blue eyes, a red moustache and blond hair. His face, white and round, had become emaciated with constant worry and long watches but yet it was inherently gay.

He had found that the *émigrés* were strongly divided among themselves as to method; whether to rely on Russia, Serbia or the west. He decided that it was essential to travel throughout Bulgaria to acquire knowledge and to inspire and organise the people for an armed rebellion. His manifesto was simple, 'by means of a general revolution to overthrow the present despotic and tyrannical system and to replace it by a democratic republic'. He looked ahead beyond the day of deliverance.

'When Bulgaria is free,' he was asked, 'who will be king?'

'If it is only to have a king that we fight the Turks,' he replied, 'We are idiots. We have a sultan now. What need do we have of a new master? We want liberty and equality.'

'But what will you do when we have won? You will have earned the top post.'

'I want nothing for myself. If I succeed, we all succeed, if I fail,

I fail alone. I will go to another people, to do for them what I am doing for ourselves.'

Everywhere he went he left an unaccustomed hope. He was 'a child of the night', visiting cottages, monasteries and cities, always gay, often singing. He had no hatred, he respected the Turkish people. Danger was his natural element. He was completely fearless; his very contempt for danger brought a certain protection.

Once at a meeting, one of the conspirators was well known to be a police informer. Levski went up to him and slapped him. 'Get out, you contemptible fellow,' he said. 'Why are you doing this to me? What have I done?' 'Clear out at once. Denounce us to the Turks. It is I, Levski.' 'Don't be afraid,' he told his companions, 'this chap is a coward. He will do nothing.'

He was not only known as Levski the lion; the peasants looked on him as a saint, calling him *Diakona*, the priest, *Daskala*, the teacher and *apostol*. He seemed to bear a charmed life. His portrait had been circulated throughout the land, his enemies were all around him. On one occasion, disguised as a beggar and with a patch over one eye, he asked a Turkish policeman the way to the doctor's. At another time, on the second day of Easter, he made the congregation sing a revolutionary song in church, to the horror of the *chorbadji*:

> Blaze up in us, oh love so bright,
> Against the Turks we'll go and fight.

He might have lived to head the uprising had he not been betrayed, for a reason that had nothing to do with politics, by a priest, Pope Krustyu, who had been found pilfering the committee's funds. He was caught in a village inn near Kukrina and wounded after a short skirmish. He spent a night in the prison at Turnovo, where I saw a prisoner's scribbled prophecy, 'here a generation is being brought up that threatens the one that put it here.' He was taken to trial at Sofia. Fearful of betraying his comrades he banged his head against the prison walls, was carried out half alive and hanged on a gibbet.

Botev, his successor, wrote *The Hanging of Vassil Levski*:

> Weep on, weep on. Near Sofia town
> A ghastly gallows I have seen standing,
> And your own son, Bulgaria
> There with dreadful force is hanging.

HRISTO BOTEV

Hristo Botev, third of the great trio, was born on Christmas Day, 1848, the year of revolutions; his birthplace, Kalofer, in the valley of roses – and of heroes.

These small towns at the foot of the mountains were poor from the Turkish point of view, communications were bad and the occupation forces were spread out thinly. There were a few rich merchants but most of the inhabitants were craftsmen in leather, woodcraft and embroidery. Hristo's father was a teacher and a scholar, known locally as something of a hothead. His mother whom he adored was a fine singer of folk-songs that awoke his patriotism and his muse. From exile he wrote one of his best loved poems to her.

> Do not weep, Mother, nor sorrow
> That I have become a *haidouk*,
> A *haidouk*, Mother, a brigand,
> Leaving you alone and unhappy
> Mourning the first of your children.
>
> But, Mother, blast with your curses
> This black Turkish oppression
> That sends us young men into exile
> To a strange land's desolation
> Unloved, unhappy, uncherished.

In 1863 young Botev was sent on a scholarship to Odessa where he became acquainted with the works of Tchernichevsky and Herzen. He returned to Bulgaria a revolutionary idealist and au utopian. His scholarship had been withdrawn by the disapproving *chorbadji*.

He took up his father's profession of teaching but on May the twenty-fourth 1867, the feastday of St Cyril and St Methodius he gathered a crowd and made an inflammatory speech. He was

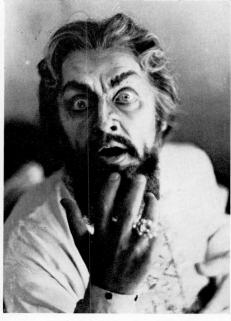

Nicolai Ghiuselev as Boris

Milen Paunov in Boris Godunov

Katya Popova as Manon

Nicolai Ghiaurov as Boris

13. Some Bulgarian singers

14. The Cherry Tree Gun at Koprivshtitsa

15. Hristo Botev

16. Vassil Levski

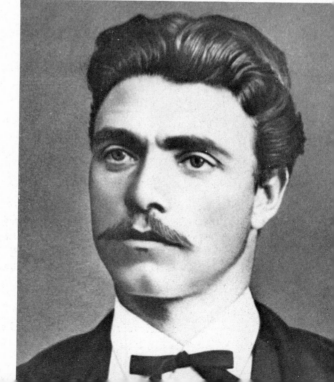

17. Plovdiv – a street in the old city

packed off abroad, first to Russia then Rumania. In Braïla he
edited a number of newspapers highly critical of the Turks. Lack
of money closed them down. He lived for one winter with Levski
in a mill outside the town. They were desperately poor and the cold
was intense. 'Whatever trouble we are in,' he wrote, 'Levski always
sings.' Vazov has given a vivid picture of these Bulgarian exiles in
his *Sans Feu ni Lieu*. He now became an active conspirator with the
plan of forming a band of *haidouti* to cross the Danube into Bulgaria, harassing the Turks and gathering recruits in the process.

In 1876 he put the plan into operation in support of the uprising
that had been proclaimed. The insurgents, in driblets, got on
board the Austrian river boat *Radetsky*, their arms and uniforms
hidden in baskets of market produce and cases of gardening tools.
At a given signal they seized the ship, changed into uniform and
forced the captain to land them near Lom. They marched on to
Vratza in the Balkan ranges but in the meantime the uprising had
collapsed and the Turks were able to concentrate all the forces in
the district against Botev's small band. After a fierce battle in
which until nightfall they threw back attack after attack Botev,
alone with a small rearguard, was killed either by an enemy bullet
or through treachery. His fate is obscure.

Botev's ideals are of particular interest in relation to the Bulgarian of today. He was a revolutionary and an internationalist with
a burning faith in the brotherhood of man. He aspired to a Balkan
Union based on communism. In 1871, the year of the Paris commune, he wrote: 'I await the awakening of the peoples and the
future communist order in the whole world.' He was not, however,
a scientific Marxist so much as an utopian of the school of Tchernichevsky and Proudhon. He disapproved of modern inventions as
benefiting the rich at the expense of the poor. He believed, however, that all literature should assume the character of political
propaganda. His own poetry was a call to action.

Botev is known and loved not only as a fighter but as one of
Bulgaria's greatest poets. He had little time and his output was
small, some twenty-five poems in all. One of his most moving
poems, *Haidouti*, is unfinished. It tells of the heroic *voevode*,
Chavdar, and 'the people that gave us wings'. Another poem, also

E

in ballad form, celebrates Hadji Dimiter, the *voevode* who crossed
the Danube with his band and was killed. In it there are his most
famous lines, engraved on his own gigantic monument at Vratza
and on so many cenotaphs:

> *He does not die who falls in battle,*
> *Fighting for freedom.* Everything mourns him,
> Both earth and heaven, wild beast and nature,
> And of him minstrels sing their songs.
>
> By day an eagle keeps the sun from him,
> And a wolf gently licks his wound –
> A falcon too, the bird for a hero
> Hovers above him, his brother true.
>
> Evening draws down, and the moon rises
> Stars bespangle the vault of the sky;
> The forest rustles, a wind awakens
> The mountain is singing a *haidouk* song.

THE POETIC MADNESS OF 1876

It is now time to return to Koprivshtitsa and to Todor Kableshkov, the owner of the superb house we have been visiting. We see
him as a young man of twenty-six, lean with a pale swarthy complexion, moustaches just beginning to sprout. A man of burning
eyes, a consumptive in a great hurry, an optimist who believed that
they had only to rise for the Sublime Porte to collapse in ruins.

Levski had been hanged; without his inspiration and abilities as
an organiser the movement was in disarray. In 1875 a local uprising
in Stara Zagora had been rushed, but Turkey was growing
weaker; *The Times* had written that Turkey's rebirth was as
impossible as the restoration of the Holy Roman Empire. The
central committee decided that now was the time.

And indeed with the approach of spring – writes Vazov – the
revolutionary ferment spread with giant strides. All western Thrace –
its chief centre – was like a volcano that spring, emitting dull rumblings that announced the coming eruption. A swarm of apostles and
preachers journeyed over hill and dale, organising the struggle. . . .
A long line of forerunners had laboured in Bulgaria's spiritual
field. . . . That glorious line, which began with Païssi, the monk, and

ended with Levski, the deacon, both of them saints . . . the first had blessed it from the heights of Mount Athos, while the second blessed it from the gallows.

Some twenty years ago, Rakovski, when he had merely hinted at revolution in a village, had barely escaped from the fury of the peasants by disguising himself in women's clothes. Today, when the people heard an apostle was coming, instead of posses, they sent deputations to meet him.

Georgi Benkovski, whose house we also see in Koprivshtitsa, overcame the hesitations of the more cautious and May the first, 1876, was fixed as D-Day. The decision was known to hundreds and a traitor, Nenko Stoyanov, a wealthy farmer, went straight from the meeting to warn the Turkish police in Plovdiv. They promptly arrested four members of the committee and sent a posse of fourteen soldiers to Koprivshtitsa to arrest Todor Kableshkov, the local leader. He was ill in bed when they came to the house. His mother delayed the captain. 'Sit down and have a cup of coffee. Todor is not at home. I will send someone to look for him.'

'I will look for him myself.'

'Why do you want him?'

'I have a letter for him.'

Hearing the voices, Kableshkov escaped by a back door and went to the house of another revolutionary. There was considerable doubt as to what to do when another 'apostle' entered and told them that he too was being hunted. Clearly the movement had been betrayed, but they believed that the organisation was still intact. The central committee had fixed on May the first, but the conspirators felt that in the new circumstances they must proceed immediately.

Negib Aga, delighted with his bag of four and confident that they would all be taken by May the first, was sipping his coffee when he heard the first shot. A Turkish soldier had been killed on the little bridge – 'The bridge of the first gun'. The conspirators captured the Turkish Konak (H.Q.) and seized the prison, killing the guard and freeing their companions, but the remainder of the Turks had succeeded in escaping to their headquarters at Plovdiv. There was a brief and deceptive period of calm and Kableshkov returned home to write and tell the central committee what had happened.

'The standard is waving in front of the prison . . . guns are being fired to the accompaniment of the church bells and brave men kiss one another in the streets. And if you have been true patriots and if you pine for liberty, follow our example . . .'

The letter was signed in the blood of the first Turkish soldier to be killed.

After five centuries of occupation Koprivshtitsa was the first Bulgarian town to be freed.

The 'blood letter' inspired the other districts to revolt and Benkovski with his flying detachment freed a large number of villages.

The Turks reacted vigorously. Botev, coming with help from Rumania, had been killed; bands of *bashi bazouks* led by a feudal war lord, Ahmed Baroutinlia, ravaged the countryside, followed by well-armed regulars. They burnt down town after town, massacring the women and children. In Plovdiv gallows lined the streets and the heads of the murdered were brandished on pikes. The name of Batak 'winged its way beyond the struggle' as, in the more civilised future, Guernica, Lidice, Oradour, Hiroshima and Nagasaki. Benkovski was killed in battle, Kableshkov committed suicide in gaol.

'The April rising was a still-born child, conceived in the infatuation of a most ardent love and choked by its mother in the throes of childbirth. It died before it had lived. It was a poetic madness. For young peoples, like the young, are poets.'* Koprivshtitsa was saved from destruction by a heavy ransom and survives today, a museum town of six thousand inhabitants, a quiet and beautiful place of pilgrimage.

We have now met a representative gathering of heroes and two heroines. They have one mother, Bulgaria. They kill but they are not killers. Without exception they are sensitive; poets and intellectuals nurtured on the warm and life-enhancing songs of their countryside. Their aim is not to destroy but to create.

They failed in their immediate objectives, all gave up their lives

* Ivan Vazov, *Under the Yoke*

and never saw the promised land. They were fully prepared for sacrifice but they did not set out to be martyrs, they wanted so much to live to enjoy a free Bulgaria. Theirs was no narrow and selfish nationalism, they dreamed of a Balkan union at peace with the world. Seldom in any period of history can there have been such a band of men and women, so innocent and selfless, hating the oppressor but always clearly identifying him, so that their hatred was concentrated and did not overflow and embitter them. It is through their direct inspiration that the uprising of 1923 and the revolution of 1944 took the forms that they did. Their successors were from the same mould, tough only because they had to be, single-minded only because they had to be, gay in moments of the greatest danger; their love was always so much more powerful than their hatred. It is because of these things they live today, not only as the names of football teams, pioneers, streets and towns or the inscriptions on cenotaphs, but in the character of the people they helped to form and to free.

I met Levski and Liliana Dimitrova in the classroom and in the street, members of the Komosomol and collectives. In Bulgaria as nowhere else past, present and future are one.

AND AT HOME: A POSTSCRIPT

It is interesting, after having relived the uprising of 1876 on the spot, to see it at a distance, from England.

Rumours of atrocities in Bulgaria had been gaining ground until J. MacGahan wrote an eyewitness account in the Liberal *Daily News*, dated June twenty-third, 1876; a strong argument for a free Press.

'Here is what I saw . . . I counted from the saddle a hundred skulls . . . all women and children . . . long brown hair hanging from the skulls . . . the whole churchyard for three feet deep was festering with dead bodies . . . three thousand bodies in the churchyard and church. We were obliged to hold tobacco to our noses.'

Also in the *Daily News*, the American consul Schuyer wrote: 'Old men had their eyes torn out and their limbs cut off . . . pregnant women were ripped open and the unborn babies carried triumphantly on the point of bayonet and sabre.' Nor was this the work of local thugs. It was directly inspired from Constantinople; the most cruel were rewarded and the few who showed mercy downgraded.

Disraeli shrugged it off as 'coffee house babble', always careful to write the word 'atrocities' in inverted commas. His biographers, Monypenny and Buckle, defending the indefensible, write, 'it was a most lurid story, decorated with extravagent particulars which it was difficult for the judicious to believe'. It is still a habit of the judicious to find so many things difficult to believe.

Let us hear Disraeli's own words, always bearing in mind that it was Gladstone who was called the hypocrite – 'I would still express a hope that, when we become better informed, I would express the hope for the sake of human nature itself – when we are thoroughly informed of what has occurred, it will be found that the statements are scarcely warranted.' He went on, 'I cannot doubt that atrocities have been committed in Bulgaria . . . but that more than ten thousand persons have been imprisoned, I doubt. In fact, I doubt whether there is prison accommodation for so many or that torture has been practised on a grand scale among an oriental people who seldom, I believe, resort to torture, but generally terminate their connection with *culprits* (my italics) in a more expeditious manner.' 'At these words,' writes the biographer, 'there was a laugh in the House, always expectant of some humorous sally in the Prime Minister's utterances.'

Almost immediately after this humorous sally Disraeli entered the House of Lords as the Earl of Beaconsfield.

Gladstone thundered in pamphlet and in words about these 'fell satanic orgies'.

'Let the Turks now carry away their abuses in the only possible manner – namely by carrying off themselves. Their Zaptichs, and their Mudirs, their Bimbashis and their Yuzbashis, their Kaimakans and their Pachas, one and all, bag and baggage, shall, I hope, clear out from the province they have desolated and profaned.'

Disraeli, again in his most jocular vein, said that this outburst was 'of all the Bulgarian atrocities perhaps the greatest'. And two years later he brought back 'Peace with Honour', handing back a province of the now freed Bulgaria to the butchers of Plovdiv and

Batak. Neville Chamberlain was to repeat the same unhappy phrase, this time at the expense of the Czechs.

Turgenev wrote his poem *Croquet at Windsor* in which the croquet balls on the lawn at Windsor turned into skulls and shocked the Queen by blooding the hem of her dress. She had praised Disraeli for his wise attitude.

Gladstone's name lives in Bulgaria today; MacGahan, forgotten in England, is gratefully remembered.

10. THE VALLEY OF ROSES

From the moment that, on the eve of my departure, I first heard the name 'Valley of Roses' I had thought of it as a compelling three-star tourist attraction, to be placed alongside the tulip fields of Holland. I could not, however, help seeing it in terms of my own small rose garden, greatly magnified and sprawling over a narrow valley, bridging streams, trailing around trees and framing cottage doors. I added a nightingale chorus to complete the picture. This vision through rose-coloured spectacles was, of course, complete nonsense since I knew that it was a commercial crop and must therefore be even more domesticated than my own few bushes.

Now I was approaching it from Koprivshtitsa, where, after passing the conspirators' pharmacy and crossing the little bridge, I felt that in the homes of Todor Kableshkov and Georgi Benkovski I had found the real Bulgaria. It had been a rewarding experience; now I was no longer a tourist in search of star attractions, I was completely at home and could look at the valley through Bulgarian eyes, first as the cradle of national independence, the valley of heroes, where every name had a deep significance and only then in the practical light of a crop that was literally worth its weight in gold. Nor did this last practical view detract from the beauty. The bushes of red and white roses are as disciplined as vines and still more beautiful. One should not see the valley in the harsh and unsubtle sunshine but at dawn when the dew glistens on each rose, when the colour is more intense and it is a picture by a pre-Raphaelite with each dew filled petal clearly defined, rather than by an Impressionist. At dawn too the whole valley is scented.

Here also are the beginnings of history with the remains of Thracian and Roman settlements all around. The Strouma river flowing through the Karlovo Valley was mentioned by Pliny and the remains of the ancient Thracian town of Seuthopolis were dug up twenty years ago during the construction of the great Georgi Dimitrov dam. The two-thousand-three-hundred-year-old Thracian tomb of Kazanluk has some magnificent frescoes.* Around the dome in the centre there is a chariot race, the horses galloping as in a painting by Géricault, and this is encircled by the funeral scene. The hand of the Thracian noble, blackened and dead, is clasped by his loving wife, on either side there are attendant slaves playing flutes and bearing household goods while others hold horses. It is a moving work superbly drawn. This then is also the valley of antiquities and of art.

To the Bulgarian the old and the new belong together and are an equal source of pride. Thracian and Roman buildings, the national renaissance and the twenty years of socialist industrial achievement, with its impressive statistical tables, together establish the identity of a people. And the rose is still an object of beauty to the harvester, the engineer and the chemist.

The valley, sheltered between the Balkan's warm southern slopes and the northern foothills of the Sredna Gora, is eighty miles long and nine miles wide. History does not record when the rose bush first came to Bulgaria. Most probably the original cuttings were brought from Persia during the seventeenth century to decorate the gardens of the sybaritic Turkish pashas, gradually finding their way into Bulgarian's gardens, eventually to become a commercial crop. The climate is perfect, warm and sheltered with some rain almost every evening.

We walked knee deep through rose petals into one of the many

* The tomb is now closed to prevent fading but the frescoes can in the meantime be seen in reproduction.

distilleries, and the engineer and members of the collective welcomed us and showed us round.

There are two types of rose, the *rosa alba* and the red *rosa damascena milla*, a more delicate flower to rear but one with a higher yield and better scent. These must be plucked between five and nine in the morning. They are then fed into giant copper vats and the precious attar is extracted and locked up, leaving the rose-water. It takes two thousand roses to produce one gramme. One of the workers told me that at first the smell is agreeable, then it becomes overpowering and nauseating and finally they do not notice it. It finds its way into perfumes all over the world, valuable not only for its own aroma but as a fixative. It has some curiously unexpected byproducts; the workers say that the rose-water is an admirable laxative, rubbed on the gums it is a cure for gingivitis and very recently the Japanese have been experimenting with the attar in cancer research. A white-coated woman chemist, surrounded by test-tubes, was testing the product of each vat by nose and analysis. She told me that as with wine there were vintage years and poor years so that skilled blending was necessary. In the office there were large round metal drums of the extract. At Kazanluk there is an agricultural research unit which grows and tests twelve hundred different types of rose. During the war the Germans characteristically made the Bulgarians grub up the plantations to avoid competition with a synthetic *ersatz* production of their own. It took five years to re-establish the plantations. The harvest festival, a picturesque affair with the workers garlanded and in national costume, takes place on June the first. As we were leaving, the chief engineer ran after us with two beer bottles filled with rose-water; the car was scented for two months and I have just smelt a piece of blotting-paper that I soaked in the water. It brings back the scene vividly.

All along our route there were also beds of lavender, vast fields of sunflowers, climbing vines and hops, and the roads were bordered by plum and cherry trees which the passers-by left unmolested. At midday the workers sat under the trees eating hunks of bread with cheese or sausage. We passed carts laden with produce and carrying groups of attractive girls back to the farm-house. For once the familiar travel posters showed the literal truth, the girls were as gay and as pretty as their pictures.

Everywhere also, a welcome anachronism in a mechanically conscious civilisation, there was the patient donkey, often carrying some old peasant in his Turkish-type costume of round fur hat, even under the scorching summer sun, and baggy trousers fastened at the waist with a broad sash. Some of the girls carried yokes (*kobilitsa*) over one shoulder, balancing rounded copper bowls (*mentsi*) of water. It was the custom, and maybe still is, for a suitor to announce his intentions by taking a sip from one of the bowls, the girl, if willing, then gives him the flower from her hair.* Nowhere in all my trips did I see a broken-down hovel or a house that was not light, airy and solidly constructed. The collective farms themselves were models of hygiene. The workers had their own plots of land where they could grow produce for their personal use. There were club houses, canteens and crèches and also facilities for art classes, dramatic performances, reading and choral societies. I did not visit selected farms but dropped in unannounced where fancy took me, always receiving a warm welcome and a drink or a meal. In the woods and forests, where cultivation ceased, the wild flowers and shrubs were as colourful and scented as in any garden. There was never a dull patch of road and the changes of scenery were rapid, from the Tyrol to the Hebrides in a quarter of an hour, from tobacco to grapes, and everywhere cattle, goats, pigs, flocks of geese and hens running free, as they should if they are to taste of anything. On the rooftops storks sat patiently on their nests.

As we passed through the valley my companion quoted Vazov's *My Dear Beloved Homeland*.

My dear beloved homeland, how beautiful you are!
How wonderful the blue of your boundless sky's broad range
With endless variations your dazzling landscapes change
New beauties, and still newer, rise at each glance,
Here lies the laughing valley, there lie afar the mountain's towers,
The sky is filled with jewels, the earth is filled with flowers!
My dear beloved homeland, how beautiful you are!

* See woodcut on title page.

The marble lion on the Shipka victory memorial looks down on the Valley of Roses. 'Everything is quiet on Shipka' said the communiqué, commemorated by Verestchagin, the once famous Russian painter of battle scenes, in his grim picture of the frozen Russian soldier. To defend the pass six thousand Russians and Bulgarians under General Stoletov, when their ammunition began to run out, hurled down rocks and the bodies of their dead to impede the Turkish army of forty thousand men. It is a hard and cold climb even in summer and a halt at the Balkantourist hotel was welcome.

11. EXCURSIONS

DONKA

I had not been more than a fortnight in Sofia on my second visit before Paunov had to leave to sing in *Boris Godounov* under Karajan in Salzburg. I would miss him but at the same time, for his sake, was greatly relieved. He is a perfectionist and he was driving himself too hard, singing and rehearsing, working at the Concert Direction as well as looking after me, and I had become very much a whole-time job. He told me that he had found an ideal substitute, a student of English in her last year at Sofia University who had translated for Ava June in the international singers' contest. Donka duly presented herself at the hotel. Her English was fluent and idiomatic. She was a little diffident and spoke in a low voice. I knew at once that I liked her, she had those sparkling about-to-laugh Bulgarian eyes, but I had some doubts as to whether she would prove forceful enough. Paunov, an admirable actor, could deal with any situation, changing his personality from the crafty Prince Shuisky to the bewildered Pinkerton or the brutal German sergeant in *Semyon Kotko* as occasion demanded. A well-known artist, he knew everyone. A walk with him down the Boulevard Rouski involved a dozen halts with an introduction, a conversation and then a brief and vivid biography of the people we had met. I felt that in his hands nothing could go wrong and it never did from that morning when we stood outside Cook's office, which was unexpectedly closed, and I threw pebbles at the window shouting 'Hi, Cook's' at the top of my voice while he went to the Polyclinic next door and got on to the phone. In a moment the office was opened. He could summon a car from nowhere; on one occasion, when we were stranded, borrowing a high official's car, his best Boyar manner overcoming the chauffeur's doubts and objections. I felt that I might well be lost without him.

I asked Donka whether, when we came to Varna, she could speak up loud enough to make my points heard among fifteen other members of the jury and their interpreters usually talking at the same time. 'I have done some teaching practice,' she said in the same quiet voice, 'and have handled a class of boys. I think I can cope.' When the time came not only did she cope with English and Bulgarian but Russian and German as well and with that rare translator's gift of being able to assume the personality of the person for whom she was translating. I have never met a more brilliant girl or a more charming and thoughtful one. She adored her country in a thoroughly informed way, particularly Sofia about which she became lyrical. Her knowledge was vast but never dryly factual; she could find an appropriate English quotation from Chaucer to Wodehouse and she was steeped in the history and traditions of Bulgaria, realising that legend, folk-lore and poetry were also important facts. This attitude was not exceptional in Bulgaria but she had it to an exceptional degree. And this learned philologist could giggle like the schoolgirl she had so recently been. My wife and I came to love her like a daughter.

That first morning we decided that we would try one another out on a trip to Belogradchik and Vidin.

'OLD YOTSO'

The countryside immediately adjacent to Sofia has a very special character, its people are the *Schoppe*, shrewd peasants with a dialect and a humour of their own, the subject of innumerable anecdotes. One such tells of two peasants who were hauling a barrel of wine in a cart. It was a hot day and they became thirsty. The wine was a strong temptation. One of them thought for a time and came out with a solution. 'It will be all right if I pay for the drink.' He took a hearty swig and handed his companion a coin. The other peasant did the same thing, handing back the coin. And so the coin passed backwards and forwards until the barrel was empty. When *My Fair Lady* is translated into Bulgarian, Eliza may well speak in the *Schoppe* dialect.

When the car came out into a narrow gorge we saw a train in the distance and heard it whistle. 'You see that rock there,' Donka said as she pointed, 'that is where old Yotso watched.'

'And who was old Yotso?'

'He was a peasant who lived in that remote village over the gorge in the desolate heights of the Stara Planina above the Iskar Ravine where we are now passing. He went blind at the age of sixty-four just before the liberation. All that he could do now was to live in the past remembering the horrors of his life as a serf, seeing in his imagination all that he had ever experienced, the fierce Turks in their red fezes, the hardness of their horses and their biting whips. He had no joy and no hope. It was a living death.

'"It is just now that I need my eyes," he thinks when he hears the glad news of the liberation. Then an official comes to the village, a real Bulgarian *pacha*. The old man is stirred. He feels the uniform, kisses the epaulettes, crosses himself and says, "Lord I have seen."

'But soon the gloom of the long night returns with its deadly monotony. He is perplexed by the petty village squabbles that he hears all around him. "They are free now," he says to himself, "and should be happy. Surely it is they who are blind and not I."

'A soldier comes to the village and tells of the marvels of Sofia and the old man clutches and kisses his sword. For a time he lives under the impression of this new symbol of freedom but as this wears off he sinks into still greater apathy, listening to the road of the river below.

'Then there come rumours of a new railway, a Bulgarian railway. "A mighty empire could not do this and we are doing it." At the first echoing blasts his eyes fill with tears.

'Daily he sits on that rock I showed you, high over the ravine, listening to the work. Then with the first rumble of wheels and the first shrill whistle he is reborn. And now when he hears the whistle he drops everything and runs to his rock. Passengers would see old Yotso waving his cape to them, his way of greeting the new Bulgaria. "Is it a madman?" they ask at first. "No, it's old Yotso watching." And one day he does not return. His son finds him there dead, cap in hand.'

'Is that a true story?' I ask.

'Of course,' Donka replies. 'It was written by Vazov.'

BELOGRADCHIK, MAGOURA AND VIDIN

We spent that night at Belogradchik in a modest and comfortable non-Balkantourist hotel. I then discovered an unsuspected hazard in ordering a meal abroad. In the mistaken idea that I could handle a menu anywhere in the world, I brushed aside Donka's aid and with a grand gesture calculated to impress I said to the waiter – '*Guvech*'.

He shook his head.

'*Mish-mash.*'

He shook his head again.

'*Kebab.*'

Yet another shake of the head and so on throughout the whole impressive list. Was it all off? I could see my neighbours enjoying a hearty meal. When Donka had finished laughing she explained what had happened.

'In Bulgaria we shake our heads when we mean yes and nod when we mean no.'

I never grew used to this inverted piece of mime. I learnt afterwards that it was the same in Turkey, so that it is an obvious legacy of the occupation.

After dinner we went to see the wonderful rock formation. Here is how the French traveller and economist Jerome Blanqui described it in 1841:

> We had hardly left Belogradchik when a most unexpected and wonderful view revealed itself before our eyes. We entered a number of narrow gorges among reddish rocks of most picturesque shapes. These rocks, almost all of them detached from one another, resembled long needles or enormous inverted stalactites, and at times they bore a fantastic resemblance to animals, ships and houses. The rocks rose to the left and right of the road very much like trees lining an alley. Most of the cliffs towered to a height of three hundred feet and seemed porous and crumbling. I saw rocks projecting out of a clump of trees . . . I invite all artists and geologists to visit Belogradchik.

Today the wonder and the beauty remain but the spectator's vision has completely altered. It has become a gigantic exhibition of prototypes for works by Brancusi, Moore and Giacometti, especially Giacometti. The Almighty has indulged in an orgy of degenerate western art breaking all the canons of socialist realism!

I visited the cliffs at dawn. The changes of light and colour as the clouds scudded by, the utter silence and a hawk gliding and swooping above brought one right into the middle of a primeval landscape by Max Ernst. Nature was copying art, a proof of Wilde's dictum.

Nature and art combine in the fantastic Roman fortress reinforced by the Turks, the stonework blending in with the rock and reached by a steep century of steps. Once inside the heavy gateway there was another hard climb and a gate that led to an almost vertical path to the summit with its massive writhing rocks. As I was seeing things in terms of painting that morning this was surely one of mad Martin's apocalyptic visions.

This seemingly impregnable fortress, which even today in a non-nuclear war would be as strong a barrier as Monte Cassino, was taken in 1850 by twelve thousand peasants; a premature victory but one that showed the spirit of the peasants and greatly inspired Levski and his colleagues.

Near by were the gigantic Magoura caves. I have had caves with their cunningly concealed electric spots lighting the guide's flights of fancy. 'This is called the lion hall . . . here you can see a dog begging . . . look up at the top left-hand corner and you will see an elephant . . .' I never do. Although the commentary was in Bulgarian I seemed to have heard it all before in Wookey and Cheddar, the Grottes de Han, in Kentucky, New Zealand and Australia.

Your cave guardian is ever a hard and eloquent worker and he waits so very anxiously for your reactions that it seems ungracious not to advance a pace or two, cock your head, screw up your eyes and accept his suggested image with the appropriate grunts of recognition.

Of course these things are beautiful, to the original explorers they must have been awe-inspiring and fearful. But now with their spotlights they seem faked and theatrical, the baroque of the film studio plasterer; or is it all done by mirrors?

I dislike too the icy drops on my bald head; thank goodness it takes millions of years to form a stalagmite.

The dank walk of nearly a mile through the enormous chill halls was rewarded in this case by the primitive paintings in bat guano depicting, economically and vividly, a series of hunting scenes, men with bows and arrows, groups of dancing women and animal silhouettes. These are cruder than Lascaux and Altamira but the magic that inspired them still works. We came out into the brilliant warming sunshine and walked over the mountain and the caves.

The roads on the whole were good and the drivers safe enough though there being comparatively little traffic they took greater risks in overtaking than at home. One rule they observed zealously, not a drop of alcohol, not even a sip of beer until the day's stint was finished. Most of them broke the monotony of driving by turning on the wireless. This could have been horrible were it not for the very melodious and truly 'pop' songs from Bulgaria, Greece, Yugoslavia, with an occasional one from France or Italy. Through constant listening the drivers had become quite expert in naming the country, the singer and the year. There was an occasional American hillbilly and Great Britain was often represented by 'My bonnie lies over the ocean', a song that is universally popular in communist countries and in the repertoire of every choir.

It was through my contact with the many drivers that I first saw the completely democratic nature of the Bulgarians. At Varna they belonged to the large car pool of the Concert Direction. They drove but they also acted as hosts. They had their place both at the large banquets and at some small affair arranged by a high official. They expressed their opinions freely on every topic, suggested dishes we might enjoy and, if it was a *diner-dansant,* invited the ladies to dance. It is, perhaps, foolish to express surprise at anything that is so natural but such social egalitarianism was not noticeable in Russia even though the driver was one's *tovarisch.* Our own driver of the last two years, Stoyan, was not only a marvel in organising us but a shrewdly observant humorist. If I asked him for seven o'clock, he always said, 'English time, Bulgarian time, or an hour or two later as with our Cuban comrades?' He soon became an expert on ballet and seldom failed to predict a candidate's chances correctly. He had driven all the singers and musicians and as an employee of the Concert Direction was involved not merely in ferrying bodies backwards and forwards but in the whole business of the Direction's cultural mission. All the drivers had this total involvement and a pride in their country that often made them spend their days off in driving one to some interesting spot.

Our driver turned off the wireless. We had arrived at the Vin Prom in a prosperous new village near Vidin. The municipal party representative in charge of cultural affairs had driven in from Vidin and the village schoolmaster who spoke admirable French was in attendance. The occasion was a wine tasting and the local wine was the Gumza of which they were justifiably proud. We sat round a big table, bottles were filled from various casks, we swallowed rather than sipped and commented in the usual manner. It might have been France or Italy, though there were the many particularly slavonic toasts – 'to peace', 'to England', 'to Bulgaria'. I drank a toast to Dionysios, shared between wine and dance. It aroused more enthusiasm than I thought it merited until one of the workers told me that it was his name and he was grateful. The wines were strong, the weakest fourteen and a half degrees, and the talk became animated. Donka was the only woman and by far the youngest there. After the way in which she coped I no longer had any doubts that she could manage a whole opera house full of international individualists.

Vidin I found enchanting and extra hospitable since the party official in charge of cultural activities accompanied us, opened the art gallery at seven a.m. and talked with enthusiasm and knowledge about the Shakespearean performances that had been given the year before. The setting was perfect, the ancient thirteenth-century castle of Baba Vida with its four massive towers, its moat and drawbridge. The wooded promenade along the Danube is worth the visit alone and there the 'blue Danube' is not its usually muddy colour but a sparkling silver and I heard the nightingale sing. This was a rare experience but the sparrows all over Bulgaria were an endless source of amusement at mealtimes as they hopped from table to table in the terraced restaurants stealing bread, sometimes squabbling over crumbs, at others carrying off large pieces in easy stages, one knocking a roll off the table, then a group dividing it on the floor and flying off to return after a few minutes to repeat the process. In half an hour I saw four large rolls disappear into the trees.

TURNOVO

Turnovo forms the perfect partnership between man and nature. The only other example I can think of is Les Baux in Provence but Turnovo still lives. Fortunately it lies roughly half-way between Sofia and Varna, so that many motorists visit it by chance and suddenly realise that they are in another century. That is how I first came across it. It has been perfectly described over a century ago by a field-marshal who had a trained professional's view of terrain and its possibilities combined with an eye for beauty.

In 1841, in his *Letters about Conditions and Events in Turkey*, Field-Marshal Helmuth Karl Bernhard Graf von Möltke – never did a name describe a man more fully – wrote:

I have never seen a town of more romantic location than Turnovo. Imagine a narrow mountain valley in which the river Yantra had chiselled out her rocky bed between vertical stone walls and runs like a snake making most wonderful and capricious turns. One of the walls

of this valley is entirely covered by a forest while the city is situated
on the other. A conical mount rises in the middle of the valley, and its
vertical rocks make it an excellent natural fortress; the river embraces
this mount like an island, linked to the town by one single rocky road,
a rock wall rising about forty feet and two hundred feet long, just
broad enough to provide room for passage and for the aqueduct. I
have never seen such a fantastic shape for a wall, and when the
Mohammedans went into the Mosque today, I took the chance of
wresting the secret of this locality by means of a photograph.

One has the feeling that in spite of his sense of beauty he would, as a true German, have shelled the city, whose secret he had wrested, without compunction.

By way of contrast the prominent Russian author Paustovsky in an essay *Picturesque Bulgaria* (Moscow 1962) writes:

> There are towns which cannot be described with any system, so complicated and picturesque is their topography . . . without a map one cannot imagine such towns. I lived there three days yet I still cannot believe in its complete reality.
>
> It is as if, long ago, an ancient play had been performed here, then the author, the actors and the spectators had died and the décors of the fantastic town had alone remained, hanging precipitously over the river Yantra for centuries, fading in the sun.

The gorge is full of lilacs and the wooden vine-covered Bulgarian houses with their projecting bay windows, clustered together, as if for support, seem to be clambering either up towards the skyline or to be tumbling into the Yantra that reflects them in ripple broken images. A few fishermen cast their lines; I never saw anyone make a catch but what a soothing occupation. The calm is only broken by the occasional shrill whistle and echoing grind of a busy little train, a seeming toy, that passes through the valley. At first I resented it but it had so definite a personality that finally it became a friend. It gave a scale to this grand panorama.

A modern architect has done the seemingly impossible in building a hotel that not only blends with the setting but has become a feature of it, as if it had been there from the very beginning. It is the ideal combination of modern and traditional. The white marble façade seen from the street is three storeyed but from the river it has six floors with terraces all round from which one can take in the whole sweep. Wooded alleyways lead down to the river.

The detail of Turnovo only reveals itself gradually. It is necessary to spend some time there, to see it in every light and to wander through its shady precipitous lanes.

It became the centre of the great uprising against the Byzantine Empire by the feudal lords, Assen and Peter, in 1185 and was chosen as the capital of the second Bulgarian kingdom (1186–1392), a rival to Constantinople itself.

Assen II's column may be seen with its proud inscription, 'I went to war against Rumania. I beat the Greek army and took prisoner the Emperor Theodore Comnenus with all his boyars. I conquered all his lands from Adrianople to Dratch, Greek, Albanian and Serbian territories. The towns round Constantinople and even this city were dominated by the Latins. They also are in the power of my kingdom and exist only through me.'

The Tsarevets hill, which was the heart of the old city, is joined to the rest by a narrow rocky ridge that was once a drawbridge and is now a favourite walk leading to the ruins of the former Royal Palace and to the patriarchal Church of the Ascension, one of the oldest of all Bulgarian churches. There is an impressive thirteenth-century square tower in which the Byzantine Emperor, Baldwin, was imprisoned by the Bulgarian ruler Kaloyan after the battle of Adrianople in 1205.

On another hill, Trapezitsa, once the home of the wealthy boyars, there are the remains of over seventeen churches. The most interesting church is 'The Church of the Forty Martyrs' where there are many frescoes including the earliest illustrated calendar in the Balkans, a departure from the traditional style. There also is the great stone column of Khan Omurtag (816–831) with its very human inscription in Greek: 'Even if a man lives well, death comes to him and another is born. May someone to be born after me well remember the writer. The name of the sovereign is Omourtag, the sublime Khan. May it please God that he live a hundred years.'

There are some impressive buildings of the second renaissance by a self-taught architect, Kolya Ficheto, the Hadji Nikola inn, built of stone and iron with a magnificent open gallery and a superb church, St Constantine and Helen. Turnovo seems to have inspired architects at all periods.

Separated from the museum city is a busy and rapidly expanding modern town. A few miles away are two appendices to Turnovo that blend into its mood.

The first, the Preobrajensky Monastery, is one of the most serene retreats I have ever visited. It is hidden in an acacia grove below some towering rocks, a complex of wooden balconies, quiet well-watered courtyards and domes with a magnificent belfry designed by Kolya Ficheto and our friend Zograf's frescoes on the outer wall of the church showing the four seasons and the four stages in the life of man. The monastery is in use and I saw the fourteen monks being summoned to vespers by an old-fashioned clapperboard shaped like a yoke, a survival of the time when the Turks forbade bells. It is here that many *haidouti* found hospitality.

The village of Arbanassi presents a baleful contrast. Every house is a fortress with strong battlements, great iron studded gates and courtyards that were dark even in the fierce sunlight. A party of students was singing 'My woods you are so beautiful', bringing warmth where there had been none.

PLOVDIV

It is impossible to analyse why some places are immediately sympathetic even before one has had the chance of getting one's bearings. You suddenly feel that this is a moment that will always be fixed in your memory and that the most trivial impressions are important. There is the wonderful sense of physical well-being and the desire to stay and to return again and again even before you have seen nothing but a railway station or a crowded shopping street. Some fanciful writers attribute this to things half remembered from a previous existence. You almost know what you will find round the next corner. I had had this feeling very strongly once before in Nancy and now it came over me in Plovdiv. And in what a romance our psychic writer could involve himself in a city with so long and troubled a history. It is to be noted that the western believer in reincarnation, usually an amiable maiden lady, will never settle for less than Cleopatra. No one will ever admit to have been a nonentity; even in the past one kept up with the Ptolemys.

There was certainly a wide choice of experiences to be drawn on in Plovdiv; it was six thousand years old. It had been occupied by Thracians, Romans, Greeks, Macedonians, Slavs, Bulgarians, Goths, Huns, Crusaders and Turks. It had undergone five changes of name. The Thracians called it Pulpudeva, Philip II of Macedon, Philipopolis, the Romans, Ulpa Trimontium, the Turks, Philbe and the Bulgarians, Plovdiv. It had long been noted for its cultural and commercial importance and its beauty. In the second century Lucian called it 'the biggest and most beautiful of all cities, its beauty sparkled like a jewel'. Seventeen centuries later, Lamartine wrote, 'situated on the banks of a river, on rocks isolated in the midst of a large and fertile valley, it is one of the most beautiful natural sites for a city that one could imagine.' As one moves from viewpoint to viewpoint, it is built on six hills, one can see the many incarnations of Plovdiv. Even though the Turks burnt it down several times, massacred and expelled the population and tried to turn it into a Greek settlement, the Bulgarians always returned. Perhaps because of that it has so strong a personality. It was a city of terror in 1876, corpses stinking and rotting on gibbets, heads on pikes and bodies of women and children sprawling on its cobbled paths. After the Treaty of Berlin it became the capital of a new State, thought up for the occasion, eastern Rumelia, an autonomous region of the Ottoman Empire, the supreme insult to its long-suffering inhabitants. But the tragedy soon turned into farce in the still remembered history of the pasha's headgear, told me with a chuckle by an ancient who had had it from his father.

'Aleko Pasha Bogordi was appointed chief governor. At any rate he was a Bulgarian national. But the great question that occupied all minds was almost exclusively as to what headgear he would wear. It was discussed for days. Was he to enter the province as a Turkish nobleman or as the head of a free State? In other words would he wear a fez or a cap?

'When the delegation set out to welcome the governor they saw to their dismay that he was wearing a fez. The chief delegate, one Nikolaev, refused to greet him. The pasha showed not the slightest surprise; he took off his fez and put on a cap. He was immediately recognised and received with the full honour due to his position. And when he drove, capped, through the city, he received an unforgettable ovation.'

Plovdiv has one old quarter intact where time has stood still and here is one of the most graciously beautiful houses in all Bulgaria. It was built in 1847, the home of one Koyumdjoglu, a wealthy business-man. Today it is the Ethnographic museum, but arranged with such taste that it remains a home. The central bow window is supported by wooden columns, the exterior is painted blue with vases and garlands in white and green. Its windows are wide and perfectly proportioned and the tiled roof is gently curved. In the interior there is a spacious oval hall with finely carved wooden panelling and ceiling and a graceful curving stairway leading to the rooms above.

A group of students from the English-speaking school was doing some project in the house and I had a chat with them. I was amazed by their accent, taught by the phonetic method. I thought of the unintelligible French of most of ours, noticed particularly by someone used to ballet terms where *couru* becomes 'kooroo' and *battement* is transformed into 'batmong'. As I went out one of them followed me into the street, 'Thank you so much for saying we speak English well, you flatter us.'

In the hotel that evening the lift boy, a student of the French school on leave, tried his French on me. It was equally good.

Near by on the Djambaz Tepé hill is the three-storey house where Lamartine lived for a time in 1833, a sick man, sorrowing for the death of his daughter in Beirut. This is how he describes the scene in the second volume of his *Voyage en Orient*, published in 1887:

... Next morning we saw the Balkans. These beautiful mountains, overgrown with forests and interspersed with villages and rich crops, are inhabited by the Bulgarians. Having arrived at the foot of the Balkans, I found all the inhabitants of the Bulgarian village of Yenikoi waiting for us there. They took the reins of the horses, surrounded our carts to the left and right, supported them, and often raised them on their arms and shoulders to avoid the wheels running into the precipice ...

I ran a high temperature and developed an inflammation of the blood as a result of my affliction. I spent twenty days on a rush mat, struggling between life and death. Admirable was the devotion of my wife who stayed by my bedside for fifteen days without closing her eyes. She often sent people to look for leeches in the marshes of the plain. At last the Bulgarians managed to find them. Sixty leeches on my breast and temples reduced the danger ... I called for Monsieur de Campians and gave him my last instructions in case I should die.

I asked him to have me buried under a tree along the road which I saw on my way here, with only one word written on the stone, the most consoling of all words – God.

On the sixth day the fever passed and I was out of danger. . . .

That is how I managed to learn the customs of the Bulgarians. They are much like our Swiss or Savoyard peasants; simple, gentle, industrious and full of respect for their priests, who are ordinary peasants like themselves. The Bulgarians make a population of several million and are steadily increasing. The women are beautiful, lively and gracious. They seem to observe their customs, although the women no longer veil themselves as they do in Turkey. The Bulgarians are fully ripe for their independence. . . . The land inhabited by them would then be rapidly transferred into a fine garden. It is only the ruthless and stupid yoke which does not allow them to cultivate their fields with a greater degree of security. They have a passion for the land.

It was with regret that I left Yenikoi with its kindly and amiable people. It is a wonderful summer resort. All the village came out with us for one league in the Balkans to see us off, overwhelming us with good wishes and blessings . . .

The picture remains true and once again a poet had more wisdom and humanity than the politicians who kept the state enslaved. On his return to France in 1834, Lamartine delivered a speech in the *Chambre* that was a strong plea for the freedom of Bulgaria; an industrious and honest people fully prepared for nationhood. Prophetically he called for a Socialist Balkans.

Two rooms of the house are devoted to a Lamartine museum arranged by *l'Alliance Française*, the rest is divided into flats. I visited one of them where a talented painter, Entcho Pironkov, lived. The wall was covered with ikons and it was obvious that though his work showed great freedom and imagination it had deep roots in Bulgarian tradition. I would have liked to have taken one home but they were too expensive. He had already shown works in Paris. The painter in Bulgaria is largely supported by State commissions but is given the opportunity to exhibit and to sell privately. I saw many paintings in the new hotels, schools and other public buildings but few contemporary works in private dwellings. Photographic realism is no longer practised but there is nothing that would pass as modern in the west or by comparison with Yugoslavia and Poland. The Bulgarian artist is a fine colourist and at his best when inspired by his own surroundings.

We sat in the open air theatre because of the beautiful linden scented night. The concert was given by some Italian pop singers, three dreary women whose feeble voices were distorted by amplifiers; even so they were from the decibel point of view, less obnoxious, if less effective than our native variety. 'I know it's bad,' said my friend, 'but it helps to pay for the good things, your ballet contest among them.' The house was full but not very enthusiastic until the appearance of a comedian whose patter consisted of cracks about the near-by city of Gabrovo, noted, probably unjustly, for its stinginess. There was the old one about the man who dug a huge pit to find a missing *stotinki* and that other one about the man who docked the cat's tail to preserve the heat as it entered and left the living-room. These Aberdonian chestnuts provoked the same delighted laughter as they always do at home. There is a great similarity of humour, from such 'bang goes saxpence' stories to the shaggy dogs, which we swapped in the interval. The Bulgarian thoroughly enjoys a good belly laugh.

Modern Plovdiv with its great industrial fair still maintains the traditions of the past.

12. THE TOURIST'S BULGARIA

I can remember not so very long ago when the French and Italian Rivieras were regarded as strictly winter resorts reserved for the very rich. It was considered that the summers were far too hot and debilitating and then there was the risk of sunstroke. Now it is the winters that are suspect and there is a saying that the best place to send an elderly relative from whom one has expectations is the south of France. I also remember with nostalgia and regret of another kind visiting a beautiful sandy Pinède in the south of France and being told in the only *buvette* in the place that there were *terrains à vendre bon marché*. It was named Juan les Pins. Since then every square inch of the coast has been built upon, beaches have been manufactured where there was no sand and exploitation has ruined large tracts of France, Italy and Spain. Monte Carlo once so glamorous and beautiful has become an eyesore. Everyman and his wife and children travel every summer in search of guaranteed sunshine and settle down on the beach smothered in scented oil until they are baked brown. If the sun doesn't do the trick, something out of a bottle will. The stay-at-home neighbours must be made envious at all costs. Sunstroke no longer exists.

It was to satisfy these new holidaymakers that Bulgaria came into the picture with a rush, a carefully prepared rush, to help the national economy with foreign currency. Today it is a major investment.

Along the whole magnificent Black Sea Coast there were no resorts; a big port, some historic remains and sea, sand, dunes and forests. The coast was infested with snakes. My older friends tell me that it was very beautiful and oh so peaceful.

Then the government sent out a team of experts to investigate; geologists, zoologists, engineers, economists, gardeners and architects. The first problem, that of the snakes, was promptly solved by the importation of thousands of hedgehogs. They devoured the snakes and avoided becoming a problem themselves by being sold as pets to the tourists. The master plan was to prevent overcrowding by situating the new resorts at suitable intervals, with many miles of virgin beaches between and to leave the places of historic interest undisturbed.

The building of three resorts was undertaken in 1955 and 1956; Droujba (Friendship) where there had been the monastery of St Constantine with its beautiful gardens and a few private hotels, Zlatni Piassatzi (Golden Sands) and Slunchev Briag (Sunny Beach). A fourth and fifth are now being planned, one of them, the biggest of all with a beach twenty-two miles long, near the exotic Ropotamo river, the home of the waterlily. It is intended to make room by 1980 for three million foreign tourists and the plan is already well ahead of schedule. I was given a vast mass of statistics, impressive enough, if one can visualise them but nothing is more impressive than these resorts themselves.

Each one has its distinctive character, like Rila, the Stara Planina and the Rhodopes, and I choose mountains as an example because these summer cities look as if they had always been there arising complete out of the sea. Droujba, living up to its name, is a peaceful garden resort retaining its monastery garden atmosphere, Slunchev Briag is built on dunes, rather like a Belgian resort in the sun. It has wide horizons, sky and sea meet in a vast expanse of light. It is for bathing and bronzing rather than strolling. Zlatni Piassatzi, the biggest of the resorts, is in the true Riviera tradition, the Riviera as it might have been. There is a great variety in the architecture of its fifty-five hotels and twenty-two restaurants, each group of hotels has its restaurant near by. There are the palaces, multi-storey luxury-looking hotels, well spaced to provide no canyons and to block no views. The finest palace of them all, with a doorman dressed like an operatic field-marshal, is the Astoria. I wondered if the authorities realised that it was named after an American plutocrat! Each room has its balcony and the constructions seem to float. The restaurants are long and terraced and rooms are often built round massive trees, as in the magnificent casino restaurant, covered in on three sides, the open side leading one to a dance terrace giving right on to the sea. This vast hall with tables on the floor and on a surrounding gallery becomes an aviary as the swallows fly in and out, settling in the trees. For some extraordinary reason they seem to be completely house-trained!

Hotels are situated at different levels, with paths through vineyards leading down to the beaches. Some of them are small like private villas, others are long and low. The variety is endless, the homogeneity complete. The whole conception is that architecture must not be allowed to separate people from nature. It must set them down by the sea and the trees and not in a grand hotel divorced from nature. It must also stress the historical association by the use of amphorae and other Greek motives ingeniously adapted.

Many of the restaurants have a special character; they are in a sense exhibition 'stunts', though the word is unfair since the character has been suggested by the landscape. There is, for instance, Kolibite, the Indian Village. This is a complex of thatched huts, set among running streams, so completely Amazonian that one is surprised that there are no crocodiles. In some of the tree tops there are platforms with tables for dinner among the branches. On an open-air stage there is a conventional cabaret performance. Adjoining it is the Gorski Kat (A Place in the Woods) a spacious hunting lodge in wood and bamboo, the tables and benches carved out of logs. Trees are growing in the centre, their summits disappearing through the roof. The perfect model for Hagen's forest home. Most attractive of all is the Vodenitsa (the Watermill), a watermill with patios on two levels. It serves Bulgarian specialities such as *Vreteno*, a grilled pork fillet with the delicious oven hot loaves, *pitka* and the thyme scented condiment *choubritsa*. The entertainment is folk and gypsy music on a very high level.

There is also a fish restaurant, the 'Goldfish', with an attractive fisherman's hut décor, right on the edge of the sea. It suggested a *réserve* on the French coast and my mouth watered. I went there twice and all I could get was grilled cod. There is some mystery about fish. The guide books talk of the tremendous variety in the Black Sea, yet it was rarely on the menu. No succulent *fritto misto*, such a feature of a Riviera holiday. I was told repeatedly that the Turks catch all the best fish in the narrows and some certainly finds its way to Sofia where in the Balkan hotel I had excellent fish dishes. In Yalta too I had found the fish both expensive and scarce. It was only on a collective fish farm, surrounded by lakes, that two years running I had an unforgettable meal of fresh fish accompanied by draughts of Misket and Dimiat in the company of the most genial of – fishermen or fish farmers?

There is one very elegant western-style bar. I mention it because there was an exhibition of works on the walls by a Polish artist, vaguely modernistic. There was a card with the proud inscription, 'Works by this artist are in the private collections of General Eisenhower and Mr Khrushchev.'

At the highest level, well hidden by the trees, there are camping sites, hundreds of little huts that form an encampment or a sort of summer village, with running water and a general store. Near-by there is a large barbecue pit. The community has its large open-air summer theatre with nightly performances, cinema or live. In addition to the hotels, that charge less for the Bulgarians than the tourists, there are rest-houses, equally well built, for journalists,

18. The ruins of St Pantokrator at Nessebur

19. The rocks and the fortress at Belogradchik

20. Vidin: the Danube

21. Sozopol

scientific workers and so on. There they can enjoy a three weeks' holiday with excellent food for a purely nominal sum.

The climate is an equable one, less hot than the Mediterranean, the bathing is exceptionally safe and there are no restrictions on beachwear, the bikini is ubiquitous. The sea is less saline and less buoyant than the Mediterranean, there are no sharks but after a storm there are some irritating creepy insects that float on the waves and nip but leave no soreness. The beach is raked and disinfected nightly. There is no sewage or oil seepage.

There are large enclosures where men and women can sunbathe in the nude. There are the usual umbrellas and vendors of soft drinks walking backwards and forwards, crying their wares and some gypsies selling polished shells and necklaces. A horrible intrusion is an aeroplane that flies low over the beach dropping leaflets advertising Bulgarian champagne and the new gaming casino. One of the joys of the communist world had been the freedom from advertising. The family groups seemed completely uninterested either in the champagne or the gambling; all that aroused the children to a wild cheering scramble was the occasional rubber ball released as a bait.

The hotels are well furnished, every room has at least its own shower. The maids are a delight, friendly and completely disinterested in tips. True comrades, they always called my wife *Tovarich* Vera. Nowhere have I ever known rooms more thoroughly scoured, their tall vases constantly filled with fresh flowers. During the harvest tourists are provided with bunches of grapes. In the reception there is usually someone who is a good linguist, especially as there are hotels that specialise in certain nationals. Newspapers are provided free.

Many of the tourists seem to be there as part of a package deal and the Bulgarians have not yet tapped the wealthy, save the occasional motorist on his way to Greece or Turkey. I asked some of the English, whose second visit it was, why they had returned. Hearty northern voices replied, 'Damn good value for money and we made friends last year. We hope to come every year.' What was interesting was their changed attitude. Most of them had considered themselves as rather daring in visiting a communist

F

country, they had heard all sorts of disquieting stories and now they were reassured. 'People just like ourselves, don't you know, and a good deal more forthcoming. No landlady who turns you out of the house all day, whatever the weather.' Even a French visitor grudgingly admitted that the food was very good. 'Et il y a un excellent petit vin.'

The majority of the tourists seem to be West Germans, Czechs, Hungarians, Rumanians and Yugoslavs, many of them with cars. It is hoped very shortly to remove the visas between Bulgaria, Yugoslavia, Rumania and Czechoslovakia. There are surprisingly few Russians, those that I saw tended to travel in large groups rather than in family units.

The habit of putting the nationals' flag on the table has grown, encouraging conversation of the 'I was in London last year but I never saw a fog' variety. Many of the student campers from the People's Republics hold a last night of the holidays revel, dancing and parading in hastily improvised fancy dress, usually bath-towel oriental. One Czech, in the company of six pretty girls, carried a placard – 'capitalist with his harem of wives'. They sang and made merry but with good-natured sobriety.

The tourists whom I questioned seemed to think of Bulgaria mostly in terms of the seaside; they knew and liked the Bulgarian but as a holidaymaker and not as a worker, save in the tourist industry. They did go on coach excursions but whether they visited the big cities or not depended purely on their point of entry.

The tourist industry comes directly under the Council of Ministers, the publicity is magnificently handled with special glossy magazines and well illustrated and informative pamphlets on every resort and with none of the fractured English so often found in these things. Mr Velichko Peychev, the public relations officer, is a master-linguist, an enthusiast who knows his job.

This has been a crash programme, conceived on a scale that might well astonish a complex of Hiltons. There are still some 'teething troubles' in the detail; the phrase was a popular one. The plumbing, for instance, is erratic, and the public lavatories even in the smart places are well below the average both in design and maintenance. Bedroom mirrors and cupboards could be better sited, there is often too much waiting for lifts, insufficient for the size of the building. Service at table tends to be slow, not altogether surprising with the vast crowds involved. In restaurants all over the world there is a very special *maître d'hôtel* syndrome, a deafness that comes on when the bill has to be settled. This can be cured by walking briskly out. If the price to be paid for prompt service is pre-cooked food, which I suspect that it often is, then let the slowness continue.

To me the very worst of the minor irritations, and at the time it became a major one, was the excessive loudness of the many dance bands, overamplified to every corner of the vast open-air restaurants. It often made conversation impossible and indeed had such volume that one could hear no music at all, just a throbbing, rhythmic ear-assaulting roar. And where there was no orchestra the jukebox, that most horrible of all inventions, scratched and bellowed, drowning the sound of the waves and the rustle of the wind in the trees. The tinny transistor too is becoming popular. One eccentric, an Englishman, held it to his ears while the band was playing; many take it on the beach. The peace of Italy has been shattered by noise. Bulgaria beware! Finally on a still night the warm scented air tends to be polluted by the smell of cooking from the many restaurants; a matter, like all the others, that can easily be remedied.

I had the distinct impression that the authorities were leaning backwards to please the tourist but had not always got a clear picture as to what the tourist really wanted. Bands galore? Certainly, but not quite so brazen. Gambling? This raises a far larger issue that I have dealt with elsewhere.

There are in each of these resorts innumerable hotels and restaurants all competing against one another yet under the same management. The competition therefore becomes a matter of pride in a job well done rather than an all-out cut-throat struggle for survival. One might imagine that this would kill all initiative but it has not done so to any extent that I could notice. There is, save in the specialist places, an extensive standardised menu but the quality of the cooking and service varied but little. There was never a suspicion of the attitude, alas not uncommon in our seaside places, 'if you don't like it here, you can go somewhere else. We're doing you a favour by feeding you at all.' At present the 'mine host' spirit still prevails.

When work kept us up late our restaurant remained open an hour longer than usual and the manager waited on us himself. It was his suggestion and there was nothing to be gained by it, except goodwill. It is hotly debated whether this spirit can continue over the years when the pride in a new achievement is no longer fresh and tips have corrupted, when three million tourists have invaded the coast. There is some talk of a bonus system to reward the very successful. This is mooted in the Soviet Union too.

When people take their holidays on the coast they always say, 'we are going to Varna'. The resorts are new, Varna has always been there. It was settled by the Thracians, taken over by the Greeks who named it Odessos and then conquered by the Romans who turned it into a fortress. Under the Bulgarians it became a busy port that traded with the merchants of Dubrovnik and Venice. The Turks conquered it in 1391. Fifty years later the Polish hero king, Vladislav III, who had beaten a Turkish army in North Bulgaria, marched on Varna but was defeated and killed in battle there. He is gratefully remembered in a small park with a recently built mausoleum surmounted by a cross. I expressed some surprise at the cross but my guide was himself surprised by my surprise. 'The man was killed fighting for us, he died as a Christian, what on earth could be put on his memorial? The hammer and sickle?' I felt rebuked and rightly so.

Today Varna with a population of one hundred and twenty thousand is Bulgaria's third city, a centre of trade and culture. It has a small opera house with an excellent company and orchestra, a superb summer theatre that can seat three thousand and a dramatic company. It has become the home of festivals; the ballet contest, a film festival and a summer opera season.

It is a city of immense charm, it has something that no new complex, however brilliantly planned, could provide, the busy life in the streets all around, the activity of the people who live there. It is well laid out with wide wooded streets, old churches, imposing new buildings dominated by the town hall, and enchanting white-painted villas as cosily bourgeois as anything in the west. The marine gardens skirting the seashore are sweet smelling and lushly beautiful, with graceful bridges spanning streams and waterfalls that run gurgling into the sea. One of the most pleasing sights at nightfall is the children's park with its merry-go-rounds and boating lake, designed by someone with a true knowledge of children. In Varna too, as in most of the cities, promptly at six pm the main streets are closed to traffic and the inhabitants stroll up and down, talking, pushing their trim little prams and greeting one another, many of them clutching ice-creams or the hot bread rings *(Gevretsi)* that are especially good in Varna.

The mayor, in appearance a Provençal acted by Raimu, is truly representative of his city. I have enjoyed many a good drink in his company, but have never, after a late night, accepted his invitation to visit him at work at six am. The road from Golden Sands and Droujba to Varna is exceptionally attractive, challenging comparison with the Corniche moyenne or the run from Sorrento to Amalfi.

There are a number of 'advertised' tourist attractions along the coast. Near Varna there are two curious sights. The first, the Petrified Forest, discovered by Captain Spratt, an English officer stationed at Varna during the Crimean War. Out for a ride one day he came across an extraordinary phenomenon, a mass of tall hollow pillars, some of them fifteen feet in height. A ruined temple, a sort of Black Sea Stonehenge? He could find no rational explanation. Today scientists believe that these are a type of nautical stalagmite dating back fifty million years when this was the bottom of the Lutsian Sea. Once again the modern eye can only grasp it in terms of sculpture, as *objects trouvés* worked on by a Henry Moore.

In the other phenomenon, The Aladja Monastery, man has adapted nature. In the sixth century Christian hermit monks, in order to escape persecution, built their cells and chapel high up in the rocks, which were reached then as now by precipitous steps cut in the rock face.

Balchik lies to the north of Varna. It was founded during the fourth and third centuries BC, first called Kruni and then Dionysopolis because according to legend the sea washed up a statue of

Dionysus. The museum certainly has a marble torso of the god among its archaeological finds. This however is not the main attraction. Balchik was formerly in Rumania and it was there that the queen, a grand-daughter of Queen Victoria, built a summer palace in the oriental manner complete with a graceful minaret. It overhangs the sea, surrounded by terraced gardens in which are rare shrubs and flowers, well-heads, fountains and streams. It is most romantic à la Robert Hichens and was intended to be so. Local tradition says that the queen built it for her young Turkish lover, a certain Hassan, hence the minaret. Others say that it was a royal nest for lovers in the plural. It was of this queen that the story is told that the king saw a man emerging from her bedroom and challenged him: 'You are either a physician or we fight a duel – Good morning, doctor.'

True or not, and so many legends have grown up around her name, she left behind her a fairy-tale castle that today serves as a holiday home for intellectual workers and their families. When the busloads of tourists have taken their snapshots, bought their post-cards and been safely packed into their buses again, the garden is calm and the magic returns. I drank a glass of *slivova* to the memory of Queen Marie, her lovers and her architect.

To the north of Varna, adjoining Sunny Beach, there is the most interesting spot of all, a three-star must. Nessebur is built on a high rocky promontory joined to the mainland by a narrow cause-way that separates the present from the past. It seems to be floating on the sea. It was founded at the end of the sixth century BC on the site of a Thracian settlement by Darian colonists from Chalcedon and Megara, who named it Messambria. In Greek and Roman times it was fortified and the ruins of the wall girdle the city. It became a place of sanctuary in which no less than forty-two churches were built. Some are well enough preserved to be of the greatest architectural interest, especially the eighth-century St Pantokrator with its superbly ornamented arches of narrow Byzantine bricks, curved in even arcs repeating the curve of the door, repeated once again in the apse and in a wonderful dome crowned with a white cornice. St Pantokrator and the other less well-preserved churches are not dead and docketed museum pieces, they are fully integrated into a busy fishing village where there are narrow streets flanked by Bulgarian houses of the last century in which the wooden top storeys, supported by struts, project over the white plaster retaining walls, providing shadow and shelter. Even the tourists, of which I was one, a fact one easily forgets, cannot rob this place completely of its isolation and calm. There is the feeling that at any moment it could float out into the sea and disappear. It attracts many painters but only Debussy could convey its atmosphere.

My Bulgarian friends, almost without exception, told me that Sozopol some fifty kilometres farther south, near the Turkish border, was still more beautiful. We made a torrid and dusty journey there and it has left a happy memory of an outing with Ulanova and her artist husband, Vadim Rindin. Our car missed us as we wandered through the village during the hottest hour of the day, neither were we cheered by a loud-speaker that echoed through the streets – interviews with Ulanova and Haskell. When finally our driver found us the restaurant was closed. Ulanova's name was fortunately an open sesame and we were served with a very welcome meal, surrounded by all the staff and a number of the village children.

In spite of this memory Sozopol remains something of a disappointment. It too is of great historic interest, as Appolonia the oldest settlement on the coast, founded in the seventh century BC by seafarers from Miletus. Its greatest claim to fame, apart from a visit by Pericles, was a gigantic bronze statue of Apollo, the work of the fifth-century Athenian sculptor Calanus. This was carried off to Rome in 72 BC by Marcus Lucullus and all trace of it has disappeared. Archaeologists are digging up interesting relics every year; the latest, part of a necropolis with coins, gold ornaments, glass and pottery. Fishermen find amphorae in their nets.

I can see why the Bulgarians love Sozopol. The old houses are intact, there are small rockbound coves and isolated beaches. Students and painters spend their holidays there, camping or boarding with the villagers. It is the last inhabited place on the Black Sea that the Bulgarian can still call his own. He is proud of the new complexes but this is his very own retreat, where his parents and their parents once set out with a certain sense of adventure and discovery now buried under the asphalt road. Soon a new resort planned near by will bring the busloads of tourists here as it has to Nessebur.

Some time ago a Hollywood combine offered a very large sum to take over Sozopol as the location for an historical epic, the grand climax of which was to be its total destruction by fire. Not to worry, however, they would remove the debris and finance a glistening modern pleasure resort to put in its place. They must have been surprised and shocked at a poor country's response.

Farther along the coast is the city of Bourgas, a busy port, a growing industrial centre and a seaside holiday place. Apart from a beautiful maritime garden shaped like an amphitheatre it has no great tourist interest.

Out in the bay is a small island, Bolshevik Island, formerly used as a prison. In 1925, forty-two prisoners made a daring escape from there finally reaching Russia, hence the name.

Bourgas is also a spa and its mineral waters were known as far back as the fourth century. Bulgaria has some five hundred springs in use since Thracian and Roman times and more are being discovered all the time. Sofia itself owed its first fame to its healing waters. This aspect of tourism is also being developed with the building of sanatoria and rest-homes and medical research into the properties of the waters. The most famous resorts are at Gorna Banya, Hissar, Velingrad, Kynstendil and Haskovo. In all these resorts Aesculapius was the presiding deity and remains of temples, votive tablets and the original foundations of the baths are being dug up. The mineral water industry is a flourishing one.

There is one further aspect of travel in Bulgaria, the archaeological. Every few miles there are evidences of ancient cultures from a few stones, significant only to the archaeologist, to picturesque ruins that stir the imagination. The artifacts are preserved in museums all over the country. On the way to the Black Sea it is worth visiting Kolarovgrad, the ancient Shoumen, and its neighbourhood. In the city itself is the large Tumbul mosque with its slender minaret, the most beautiful in Bulgaria, and near by are the ancient capital cities of Pliska and Preslav, with impressive remains second only to Greece and Italy. There too is all the excitement of continuing discovery. It was at Madara that I saw a work of outstanding majesty, well worth a considerable detour. It is a carving representing a lion hunt, on a vertical one hundred foot cliff. The figure of the rider has suffered through erosion but the silhouette reveals a proud, even triumphant rider, his spear transfixing a lioness. The slow gait of the horse after the chase and the wearied dog, tongue hanging out of its mouth, show great sculptural quality and an extraordinary sense of observation. The Madara Horseman, seen when the sun brings it into sharp relief, is tremendously impressive. The carving is still something of a mystery to archaeologists. It was certainly allegorical of Bulgaro–Byzantine relations and the whole cliff with its inscriptions in Greek, too worn to be read clearly, is a record of the Khans of the ninth century.

PART TWO

The Bulgarian at Home

13. TEENAGERS AND ADOLESCENTS

NEGATIVE AND POSITIVE ATTITUDES

My original attraction to Bulgaria had been the quality of its young people. This was not just a question of their knowledge or their manners but of something fundamental, their whole attitude to life. They could be said to have a certain dignity and wisdom with no loss of the gaiety and sense of adventure natural to their age. In no other country have I found this so much in evidence. There was no feeling of antagonism between themselves and their elders or of speaking a different language. None of this, 'you made a mess of things and now it is our turn', so prevalent an attitude with us, fostered or tacitly accepted by many of the older generation themselves, in their fumbling efforts to be progressive. Nor was there the opposite, 'Don't argue, your parents know best'. The unfortunate word 'teenager' was unthinkable. There were obviously problems of adjustment and I was interested in discovering how these were tackled. I had spent most of my working life with adolescents so that the basic problems were familiar ones.

But, once again, let me make it quite clear, my investigation was, as far as politics were concerned, an objective one; communism as such neither repels nor attracts me, it can either be well or badly applied, truly idealistic or as grossly materialistic as the worst excesses of capitalism. Our own weakness, now that the religious ideal has so largely been broken down, is that we tend to be an aimless society with a largely negative viewpoint.

All over the western world attention is focused on the unfortunate 'teenager'. For the past twenty years he has been viewed as someone of importance who creates a vast new market for consumer goods. Advertisements are directed at him. He himself is advertised. 'Teenager', itself a copywriter's word, has become dramatised to such an extent that it has now come to have a strongly emotive meaning; 'teenage' precedes the word 'problem'. Religious discipline has largely disappeared, in too many cases whittled away by the churchman himself, and with it the words 'right' and 'wrong'. A psychoanalytical approach, commercialised and only half understood, has assured people not only that right and wrong do not exist but that it is normal to hate one's parents, or, at best, not abnormal. Parents and state have become identified, hence unrest on the campus. Samuel Butler's *The Way of All Flesh*, a sensation when it was posthumously published in 1903, revealed the damage caused by a hypocritical and overbearing Victorian parent. Today we read it as if every father had been a Reverend Theobald Pontifex, and pride ourselves smugly on our tolerant attitudes. It was an exceptional book, but today there is a flood of books, films and plays, particularly in the USA, dealing with such unhappy parent and child relationships; the exceptional has become the commonplace.

In America, and to a far lesser extent over here, the psychoanalyst has proved a poor substitute for the old time parish priest and, God knows, many parish priests were far from following the example of St John Bosco. He too often draws attention to a problem, exaggerates it and generally fails to provide a remedy. The teenager is given no protection and discipline and restraint have become ugly words. So much so that today we are surprised when a Bank Holiday is not upset by hooliganism, and the very word hooligan has been softened into 'mod', 'ted', 'rocker' or 'beatnik'. Magistrates use a headline-attracting phrase, some people blame the publicity itself, others broken homes, yet more talk of a misguided sense of adventure. In addition there is the much advertised drug problem, with some, who should know better, maintaining that reefers are not addictive and should be permitted. These are negative attitudes.

I realise that I am dealing with a minority, though a considerable one. This is not a wholesale condemnation of today's adolescents, whom I admire, but of the atmosphere that surrounds them and pushes them to rebellion.

In the communist countries the teenager is given a positive set of values and a right and wrong do exist. The aim of the education is to make him a good citizen and the way to do this is to make a good communist of him.

Pavlov, not Freud, provides the psychological basis for education and he differs sharply from Freud. He maintains that the 'determining element of mental activity is not the lowest level, the human "instinct", but the highest system, the speech system.' This agrees with Marx, 'Language is the direct reality of thought'. Consciousness and not the Unconscious plays the leading role in man's psychic life. Pavlov has no faith in all-embracing systems or speculation but in an endless series of objective experiments. Already great advances have been made in the teaching of mathematics, to take but one instance. Pavlov versus Freud is an important factor in any consideration of communist education, whether of children or adults. Pavlov is studied in school and university.

It would be a dangerous oversimplification, as I very soon realised, to believe that the State takes over completely and is the substitute for the Victorian conception of God, the portly, bearded, jealous and humourless tribal chieftain. There is a consistent series of influences; the parents' teaching and example, the kindergarten, the classroom and those specifically communist institutions, the Pioneers and the Komsomol. These cannot, as has so often been done in the west, be equated with the fascist *ballila* or the Nazi Hitler Youth and Strength through Joy movements. Both the aim and the content of the education is completely different. In Russia, during the civil war period and the Stalinist terror, there was a fierce struggle between parent and State for the possession of the child's mind, often with ugly results in which all three were the losers. Today, certainly in Bulgaria, it is no longer a struggle but a collaboration.

My first few hours in Sofia I had a long talk with a non-communist former business-man at the rehearsal of a gymnastic rally in a vast stadium. 'I am too old to learn new ways but the result is excellent. As you can see these young people have discipline but they are not intimidated. They march and they sing like free people. They have a purpose in life. It is peaceful and creative and the family unit is as strong as it has ever been in this country.'

These youth displays, semi-athletic, semi-artistic, are in a sense propagandist. They are a shop window for the youth of a nation reborn. The stress is not on strength but on the combination of discipline and gaiety. The result is graceful. The essence of this attitude can be found in the neo-classical-athletic choreography, so popular in the Soviet Union in such dances as *Spring Water* and the *Moshkovski Waltz*. There is nothing militaristic here, and if these great rallies have their propagandist aspect, it was obvious from watching this rehearsal that the gaiety was very real and that these were social occasions in which young people from all over the country came together. There was no need to tell them to smile.

Bulgaria has not only profited by the Soviet experience but has adapted it to the historical background I have outlined and to the special needs of a small country. The process of adaptation continues. There can never be a Utopia and the authorities are realistic enough to understand that utopianism is a dangerous word. Through the years of struggle, spiritual and material, has come the realisation, always to the forefront in Bulgaria, that, while the aim of their education is to create a good citizen of a communist State, the State itself only has a *raison d'être* when it belongs to and serves the individual. Now that its foundations are secure, the super-State for its own sake is becoming a worn-out conception. *L'état c'est nous*, our gymnasts seem to say.

It is from these attitudes that we can learn with profit, always remembering that education means the fitting of a person into a specific social environment and is not for export.

The first thing I noticed was the universal feeling of gratitude in the young for the education they were receiving. Nothing was taken for granted; Welfare State had no disparaging connotation of getting something for nothing with no effort required. On the contrary, it presented a challenge. It is because of this deep feeling of gratitude that the ordinary people, quite apart from any official reactions, look on defection with such disgust. 'He has taken everything and is not prepared to give anything in return.' They quote our expression 'it isn't fair play' and find our brain-drain problem a deplorable one even though the circumstances are dissimilar. Written down, as they often are in official publications, many of the things these adolescents said might seem smug; for a long time, at a distance, I discredited them. The gist of all their remarks was, 'so much has been done for us that we want to repay it'. Neither were they uncritical in their gratitude. They were intensely interested in the whole process of education, pointing out where some experiments had failed and making suggestions for future improvements. They were highly articulate. I have seen it written on many occasions that the young Bulgarian is politically apathetic. If this means that he is not interested in party politics, that of course is obvious under a one-party system. He is, however, very politically conscious with dialectical materialism as a part of his education.

I disagree also with those writers who say that the young are disillusioned with their government and with the close links with Russia. I saw no trace of this. There were the normal grumbles, mainly from housewives, at the cost of living, there was also a strong tendency to deprecate the over-emphasis with which achievements are acclaimed. These young people are highly intelligent, very well educated and exceptionally mature. They are intensely proud of their country. Naïve over-emphasis defeats its own object. Now also that there is so much contact with the west accounts of the non-communist world will have to be presented with greater objectivity or, shall we say, greater subtlety. At present, by way of reaction, the west tends to be over-idealised. I am convinced that whatever the temptations of material benefits not one of the young people I met would leave a country that they love so passionately, and the word is not an exaggeration. The relationship between professors and pupils was a free and easy one, even when the professor was held in high respect as an international celebrity. The work was hard, the syllabus in some cases overfilled but nervous breakdowns were rare and suicides through disappointment and overwork unknown. What I found particularly interesting was not so much the formal education as the various character-forming innovations. Paradoxically, their aim has something in common with our public-school education at its very best, a system not always renowned for its democratic tendencies. It would be folly to destroy and not to adapt it. But first a word about the education itself.

In Bulgaria education has always been valued as the spearhead against aggression, the most precious symbol of identity. Cyril and Methodius went into battle with the *haidouti*, the men of action were scholars, to teach was in itself a positive act of defiance. It is not by coincidence that Koprivshtitsa, renowned for its pioneer schools, was in the forefront of revolt. The slogan has never been, 'the educated man gets on in life,' but 'the educated man is a free man'.

'The importance the Bulgarians attach to education, and the efforts they have made to secure it, are very remarkable. There is scarcely a village, certainly not a large one, without a school. Those in the towns accommodate as many as five hundred or six hundred children and are conducted by five or six teachers, all of whom speak at least one foreign language,' wrote the Fourth Marquis of Bath immediately after the liberation.

Therefore with the liberation, in spite of emerging overnight from feudalism into the modern world, Bulgaria had laid an admirable foundation. This has been built on since the revolution. Last year more than one million five hundred thousand children attended elementary and secondary school and 90 per cent of primary school children went on to a secondary school education, the highest rate in the world today. Out of every ten thousand persons one hundred and twenty-two attend college or university, more than 30 per cent receive State scholarships and many others scholarships from various enterprises. After the USSR and the

United States, Bulgaria occupies third place in the proportion of university students. Illiteracy in the under fifties has been wiped out.

Compulsory schooling begins at the age of seven, before that the child can go to kindergarten. The kindergarten system is a highly developed one. There are day kindergartens, half-day ones, weekly ones, seasonal ones and special sanatoria kindergartens for delicate children. The children fall into three categories and are grouped into classes according to age; three to four years, four to five years and five to seven years. Most of the primary schools have a kindergarten attached for the pupils who are to enter the following year. I visited a number of them and was very impressed by the hygiene and by what was done to develop musical and artistic skills. The houses were small enough to provide a home nursery atmosphere. At present 74·4 of pre-school age go to kindergartens.

Secondary education begins at eleven and is compulsory up to the age of fifteen.* At the age of twelve Russian is introduced into the curriculum and from fourteen German, French or English. If the work record is satisfactory, more advanced specialised education begins at the age of fifteen. The pupil can go on to a *gymnase* for three years or to a technical school from two to four years, and then from the *gymnase* or four year technical school to the university. There are special *gymnases* for four years study in a foreign language.† After school leaving there is a maturity examination in all school subjects, unless the mark is five or higher, six is the maximum, then follows a university entrance examination.

Every week there are two hours of physical culture, either folk dancing, athletics, gymnastics, volley or basket ball.

The curriculum has been criticised, as in France and other continental countries, for being overcharged. I saw a caricature in which the whole family revolved round a small bespectacled boy, almost hidden by massive tomes doing his homework.

The enthusiasm for foreign languages is so great that the public

---

* There is an average of twenty-four children for each primary school teacher, nineteen children for each secondary school teacher.

† French schools in Varna and Sofia, German in Bourgas, Lovech and Sofia, one English in Plovdiv and Roussé and two in Sofia, Russian in Sofia and a Spanish school is soon to be opened there.

does not like dubbed films. The subtitle and the language of origin are taken as an admirable way of acquiring a language.

Here, however, I am concerned with education rather than instruction. First of all there is the traditional closely-knit family unit in which every member has a clearly defined role. We have already seen the importance of the mother in the education of the hero. There is however a total absence of the transatlantic sentimental 'mummery', the dear old lady who sits at home knitting and who is rewarded at Christmas, birthdays and mother's day by a present and a multicoloured card with a suitable printed sentiment; nor is it a matriarchy. There is enough of the oriental in the Bulgarian for father to be the natural boss in his own home. The economy demands that the mother works and that, as we shall see, is a problem placing a serious limitation on families, even though, unlike our western society, it is on the way to being properly organised. The grandparents have a positive role to play, every organisation has its crèche and hours of work are so adjusted that the mother-child contact can exist. There are no cases of children returning to empty houses and thrown on their own resources, wandering in back alleys and playing in the streets. It is true we are dealing with a country where crime, especially crime of violence, has always been minimal, as every visitor to Bulgaria for the past century has noted. For instance, this from Robert Walsh, Chaplain to the British Embassy at Constantinople in 1828, 'Crime is unknown among them; and the traveller who passes through their country is not only secure from the effects of vice, but experiences the kindness resulting from the most amiable virtues.' This was written at a period when travel in eastern Europe was dangerous.

Throughout the communist world the adolescent receives a carefully studied 'tribal initiation'.

THE PIONEERS AND THE KOMSOMOL

The Pioneers and the Komsomol have sometimes been compared by the well intentioned to our cubs and scouts. There are but few points of comparison. All children belong to these movements, the pioneers from seven to fifteen in their smart uniform of dark blue or black dress or trousers, white blouse and red cravat, then the Komsomol up to twenty-eight; thirty for office holders. It is then possible to apply for party membership which may be granted after a period of probation.

It will of course be said by some that this is a case of 'catch them young and brainwash them'. I would not argue with that point of view but it seems to me as natural for these children to be brought up as communists as for our own to swear an oath of allegiance to Queen and Country. 'Brainwashing' in citizenship, if one must use the term, is surely no evil.

I was interested and greatly impressed by the Pioneer movement, both in the USSR and Bulgaria. Broadly speaking it is a schoolchildren's club for extra-mural activities. If a child has a particular hobby, it can be cultivated under expert tuition; dancing, singing, painting, musical gymnastics, wireless and engineering, chess, gardening, languages, folk-lore; the list is a long one. Their motto is 'Always Ready'.

In Leningrad (I quote the Russian example because I was there at the right season, but the model is the same in all communist countries) I went to the Palace of Pioneers, shown round by Natasha, the nine-year-old daughter of some friends. It was her idea as an impromptu treat for me after I had taken her to the cinema. The club was a former palace, the Annichkov Palace, a spacious and very beautiful building. Rooms were set aside for every activity. There was no noise, no litter and no scribbles, damage or carved initials on the woodwork of an historic building. In some of the rooms instructors were in attendance, teaching dancing, gymnastics, but with a different attitude from school. The children had opted for these subjects and were free to opt out. Natasha, my young guide, clutched me by the hand and took me from room to room, interrupting a class to introduce me to the teachers as 'my English *dyadya* (uncle)'. In many rooms there was no teacher and the pioneers were playing chess, reading or sewing. There was always the realisation that this was their organisation and theirs the responsibility. Some were responsible for a Pioneer's park, it was faultlessly kept and shown to me with great pride. The children kept one another in order as a prefect might in a public school but by an appeal to reason and not by force. There was no trace of regimentation. If this was brainwashing, it was of the right kind for the age-group concerned. One could not wish to see happier children.

In Bulgaria the pioneer groups are named after the great heroes of whom I have written. Hero worship, so natural in the young, is fostered. The heroes are not television, pop or screen stars, not even sportsmen, though sport, especially football, is relished, but those people who built their nation, some of them communists but by no means all. 'The cult of personality' of an active politician no longer exists in Russia or Bulgaria. The whole movement is designed to combat a negative attitude, to foster a vocation and to banish boredom. The Victorian adage, 'Satan finds some mischief . . .' is very much believed in. This society has many Victorian features in its moral attitudes. The communist, the Russian much more than the more down to earth Bulgarian, often implies that he is 'not amused' by an off-colour joke.

I saw many pioneers camping or on outings, it would be difficult to imagine a friendlier or more lively bunch of children. In a very language conscious country many of them came up to me and spoke a few words of English, mentioning Robin Hood, Mr Pitkin, Winnie the Pooh and, in one case, 'you know Arsenal football club?' A little girl sang Jingle Bells and other nursery rhymes; singing is obviously a very natural means of communication. If there is a suspicion of the west in these countries – and obviously there is – it is treated impersonally, there is certainly no education in fear or hate, these are negative and the words friendship and peace are given a positive meaning. The Balkans know too much of war; they have made the distinction from the very beginning between the Turks in Turkey and the Turks in an occupied country. I saw one little Turkish pioneer, Osman, who was obviously a great favourite in the playground.*

The Komsomol continues this character education. It combines the functions of a student's union, a youth club, a marriage

---

* Before 1944 the Turks were second-class citizens. Now Osman has been given the right to be taught in his own language and to read publications in Turkish.

guidance council, a literary institute, a political club and a finishing school. It teaches the teenagers the art of self-government through the technique of meetings and organisation. Discussion is free and votes are taken. The greatest disgrace is expulsion, also taken by a free vote, in which the accused has an opportunity of defending himself.

I heard of two cases. In the first a youth had written to an American pop singer telling him that he was secretary of his fan club in Bulgaria and asking for records. The fan club was non-existent. This was considered both dishonest and anti-social, fan clubs in themselves showing a false set of values. He was expelled but has since been reinstated. Expulsion is its own punishment. The expelled person is neither sent to coventry nor ostracised in any way but misses the corporate life of the community. In the other case, a girl was accused of promiscuity with foreigners, the case was not proved and she was saved by a narrow majority. The Bulgarians have always been noted for their chastity, parents are strict in this respect, and the 'good time girl' is resented by her fellows. The Bulgarians admire the English sense of 'fair play', which they quoted on so many occasions, coupling it with the name of Gladstone!

An equally admirable institution is that of the work brigade. For about twenty-one days school parties go to the farms and help with the various harvests, boarding with the peasants. I asked the question, 'with so many aiming at higher education is there a danger of the country being split into two classes, intelligentsia and peasantry?' It was admitted to be a fair question that had to be answered. The general opinion was no. 'These brigades provide a contact that keeps us in touch with one another. The peasants are no longer illiterate so that there is no question of speaking down to them. The collectives have their musical and dramatic organisations and are not out of touch with cultural activities. Television also has become an important factor. In any case we Bulgarians are essentially an earthy people.'

In Kazanluk one night I saw a brigade gathered for briefing in the main square. There were songs, plenty of laughter and the pep-talk of the usual 'play the game' variety was kept to a bare minimum. Then the town band played, with much brass and percussion. After exams this tomato picking was obviously something of a treat. The work is not paid for at the ordinary rate. The students earn their keep and a little extra pocket money, which is increased if they do more than the allotted task. The work is not hard and there is plenty of time for recreation. Whether it is efficient in itself I do not know.

Brigade work is not always manual; it may also consist of taking part in a research project or doing translation work. Part of the school curriculum provides for a short spell in a factory. The most brilliant student I met, a philologist, was a competent turner.*

In this way education is complete and also the nation is knit together.

In spite of this educational build up, and it works, there are of course juvenile delinquents. There had been a 'teddy boy' outbreak in Sofia a few years back. They are dealt with rapidly, firmly and without publicity and are not allowed to regard themselves as heroes or martyrs. They are sent to approved schools with a normal academic programme but they are kept busy with hard practical work, brickmaking for instance. There are no bars and trust rather than force is used in rehabilitation in accordance with the Russian Makarenko† system. Given a good brain the rate of rehabilitation is high. I saw a group from one such approved school, camping for eight days in the Balkans as a reward for good work. They were not distinguishable from any other youth groups.

I asked one student if he did not become bored with political indoctrination in school. 'Yes, often,' he replied. 'I have gone to sleep at times when it was badly taught, as in every other subject. The repetition of slogans is a dangerous thing. It could alienate the

---

* The headmaster of the Wenman School at Thame, Oxfordshire has recently encouraged the experiment of letting his fifth formers out of school on Tuesday and Friday afternoons to join factory workers, office girls and shop assistants at their various jobs with the aim of giving them a greater understanding of the outside world.

† Anton Semyonovich Makarenko (1888–1939), Soviet teacher and writer who organised the redemption of the *bezprizorny* (vagabond children) in the 1920's. His account was published in England as *The Road to Life* and was also made into a film. His theory stressed the integration of the rebel into the community. Similar 'Boys Town' experiments have been tried with success in the USA.

best brains. In my case they were preaching to the converted. What is interesting is the sense of the continuity of history one gains. I do not feel that I just happened on the scene and that it is all a hopeless muddle. I know that I am lucky to have been born in Bulgaria at the present moment.'

The main danger, and it has recently been stressed by the Press in the USSR seems to me to be only indirectly due to an orthodox indoctrination; it is that of a wrong emphasis; 'materialism and the loss of spiritual values,' I quote directly from a recent issue of the *Komsomolskaya Pravda*.

What one might call the communist 'age of innocence' has passed. It had a strong puritan tinge. It could only exist in complete isolation. In Bulgaria in particular floods of tourists invade the country every year, a substantial number from the west. The aim is for three million tourists by 1980, to be temporarily absorbed in a population of eight million. This means that the majority of the nation will have some contact with the visitors, an excellent thing in itself; the main benefit of travel. It also means the introduction of a totally alien way of life that could arouse envy and dissatisfaction, since it reveals a partial and distorted picture. Even though travel is cheap it is not for everyone. People on holiday are free with money and tip largely, their clothes and their goods can arouse envy, a few behave rowdily and, because they are guests, get away with it. Italy is in the other camp, but a number of Italian films have shown the seaside wastrel, so far removed from the Komsomol idealist, carrying on temporary and ardent love affairs with the summer visitors. It has become a serious problem.

To my mind the most dangerous complication came into being in 1964 by a major blunder on the part of the authorities. This was the introduction of gambling casinos on the Varna coast. I was assured that the great safeguard was that this was only for foreign currency and would not touch the Bulgarians. In a way this seems to make matters still worse, through arousing envy, already a national characteristic as I was told so many times, and making the acquiring of foreign currency an objective in itself. Up to the present the beaches have been popular family holiday resorts with tourists and Bulgarians meeting on easy terms. The attraction of gambling will let in the 'spivs' and 'wide boys', the very element against which the whole communist education has been directed. The gambler chucking about his weight and his winnings becomes a hero, something for nothing an ideal. I was told that it was the tourist agencies, especially the English ones, who had insisted on the necessity for this and that consequently it was in the interests of the national economy. I remain convinced that it is a dangerous, totally inconsistent and short-sighted policy.

Another possible danger is the gradual introduction of 'pop' music and not, of course, on aesthetic grounds, whether these exist is a matter of individual taste, but for reasons more subtle. It was the subject of much discussion in which I often felt the matter was not clearly understood. My friends had never witnessed the concert hall and airport mass hysteria or heard the 'highbrow' apologia; they have an *intelligentsia* and have yet to develop 'highbrows'. Ban it, as was once done, and you create an immediate demand for 'forbidden fruit'. In any case the tape recorder has made it easily available.

The first danger is that it will drive out the traditional life-enhancing folk music. I remember a bitter diatribe from Jacques Prévert on the damage American 'pop' music had done in edging out the French *chansonnier*, the creator of the Parisian folk-song. We have already had innumerable examples of the positive value of this national music in breeding poets and heroes. It belongs to the people, the lyrics are true poetry and not senseless noisy jungle jingles. The other danger, more remote at present, since it is conditioned by the powerful advertising of a capitalist society, is that of the cult of the singers themselves, the glorification of the untrained amateur who suddenly finds himself rich overnight, who is neither voice-trained nor equipped to play a musical instrument, if the electric guitar can be called a musical instrument. The Beatles were known, and rightly found sympathetic, the Yeah, Yeah song was popular, but the hysterical screaming was regarded as the aberration that it is and the award at such an early age of the MBE was looked upon as yet another sign of western degeneracy. Its equivalent of 'honoured or people's artist of the republic'* had to be earned the hard way after years of professional training and public appearances.

The foreign visitors demand it, they say. It may yet prove an expensive price to pay for tourism.

What so many of the young people wanted was an opportunity to travel in the non-communist world. It should be encouraged. From inquiries I have made at the English end, collaboration in making such student exchanges has sometimes proved difficult. Currency, of course, is a hindrance. If the education has been sound, the few possible defections would be a very small price to pay. Now that the contact has been made in such a big way some exchanges at student level would correct the impression made by only seeing tourists. Like Yevtushenko, they would wish to

> hop from bus to bus like any Cockney
> and know the smell of Paris in the early dawn.

THE END PRODUCTS: THE PARTY AND
THE NON-PARTY MEMBER

The end product of this system of indoctrination, and no one would be ashamed of the word, is to produce a good communist, just as from the Middle Ages to the Victorian era it was to produce a good Christian. In neither case does it mean that the end product is intended to become a party member or a priest. For both, and there is a certain similarity though it must not be pushed too far, a vocation is necessary.

In Bulgaria there are only five hundred and fifty thousand party members. What exactly is their position and their function?

I often asked the questions, 'does the party member enjoy a privileged position? Is he in fact the founder of a new aristocracy?' The answer was always the same

> Certainly he had a privileged position in the days immediately after the revolution. He had played an active role, had risked his life, proved his right to leadership and thoroughly deserved it. At the present time it depends far more on the character of the man himself. Some, comparatively few, chuck their weight about and are not by

* There is also a high distinction for the manual worker, 'Hero of Socialist Labour'.

any means taken at their face value, the majority we respect because they are working hard in our interest. In the limited sense that they are constantly thrown together they are a society within a society, and they form a ruling class. They certainly do not earn more, in fact often less for the work they do. Your use of the word 'aristocracy' is an interesting one. There has been much criticism both in and out of the party about the attitude and behaviour of some of the children of party members who, more in the Soviet Union than here, often assume that they have hereditary privileges. This is being discouraged.

Here a listener chipped in. 'You said "ruling class"', turning to the last speaker, 'we are the ruling class, you and I. This isn't Portugal or Spain. Nobody could rule here without the will of the people. Tsankov tried it, the king tried it, and it didn't work. They are our watchdogs, our watchdogs.' He was proud of the formula.

Much of this I could confirm from my own observation. There was the fussy cock-sparrow type of man, eager to let one know that he belonged to an *élite* and incapable of making a simple statement without a portentous turn of phrase made up of the current communist clichés that are as trying and meaningless as 'Persil washes whiter' and tend to alienate the well-wisher. The vast majority, who I learnt were high up in the party, were highly cultured men of the world with a sense of obligation rather than privilege. Being Bulgarians they were tolerant and could laugh at themselves. It was the difference, if both parties will forgive the comparison, between the aggressive convert or the village dictator priest in a backward country and the scholarly Benedictine or Jesuit. Such religious parallels inevitably come to mind.

Sometimes I put the question in a slightly different form. 'Is it a handicap not to belong to the party?' Again there was much agreement.

'Less today than some years ago, and in many jobs not at all. If a man is good at his job and has something positive to offer the community, he is needed and is given the opportunity to succeed. This is a small country and we must use all the brains available.'

I met many, especially university professors and doctors, who had been put into cold storage in the torrid Stalinist days, often unjustly and with considerable hardship but who had been gradually reinstated. The commonly held view was that everyone must be a patriot and work for a common object, the general good of the community. Therefore it clearly follows that to be an anti-communist was to be a heretic and heresy was a sin. The heretic was not burnt but was certainly deprived of the opportunity of spreading opinions that could lead people into sin. Once again the religious language comes naturally.

Certainly, when one looks at the violent post-war political record of Bulgaria's neighbours, Greece and Turkey, the Bulgarians may think this suppression of heresy a small price to pay for security. Fortunately this is a choice that need not be made in England where the opposition prides itself on being 'loyal' and where most of the time half the public thinks the prime minister of the moment either a nincompoop, a knave or both with no damage done. This is not inserted out of smugness but to insist once again that to think that there is only one possible system of political life, suited to all historical backgrounds and racial temperaments at a given moment of time, is a dangerous fallacy.

I put a further question to my friends. 'Is it a handicap to practise religion?' Here the replies had much greater variety.

'I don't know. There were no believers in my faculty during my time at the university.'

'Yes, it would be a handicap for the ordinary person but not for the exceptionally gifted.'

'It might be regarded as eccentric, much like being a Mormon or a Jehovah's Witness in your country, for instance.'

'It all depends on the type of job; but of course, in one sense it would be a handicap at all ages, as it would tend to isolate one through limiting so many communal activities.'

'It is not discussed except with foreigners like yourself. It is a closed book. The word God is used but no longer with a capital letter. The Church is a museum, the repository of a past culture and to be respected as such.'

The word repository reminded me that I had seen some religious stores in Sofia with the worst kind of bleeding hearts and other pietistic images. Whether this was a subtle form of anti-religious propaganda or not, and of course it was not, it served its purpose well.

The older people, already set in their ways, said that they found it no handicap at the present day. One, a devout Orthodox, told me, 'I think it is all to the good. It distinguishes between the true believers and those who go to church through habit. There is absolutely no persecution but the education is definitely atheistic, not crudely as in the past, but scientifically. My own children are not believers and I have left them free to make their own choice. I think, indeed I am sure, that there are many more agnostics around than died-in-the-wool atheists.'

A monk told me, 'persecution might help our cause, but it would create a painful dilemma. Most of us strongly uphold all that has happened in Bulgaria; we have a wonderfully progressive tradition and we risked our lives on the same side of the barrier as the communists. We respect one another.'

Another monk, replying to the above, 'I think we are the more broadminded; we approve of them more than they approve of us. As a philosopher I can understand the agnostic position but not an atheistic one.'

And finally an interjection that delighted me from a burly priest who had been growing tired of the discussion; 'it all boils down to this; we mind our business and they mind theirs. Things work best that way.'

I felt that, perhaps, I had not minded my own business.

There is no longer a militant atheism though there are those who hate the Church and occupy an old-fashioned Colonel Blimp attitude, reminding us once again that one can equate the old party member's viewpoint with extreme Toryism. The Bulgarian is not mystical by nature and in the villages in particular there have often been cracks at the clergy such as the proverbs, 'I'm full like a priest's child on All Saints Day', or 'Tie up the priest and the village will be at peace.'

While I am on the subject of religion it is interesting to look at it from the family point of view. Many completely non-religious families keep up some kind of Christmas festivity, though there has been a shift to New Year, with a tree and with Father Frost as the presiding genius. In 1964 in the paper *Folk Culture* there was an interesting debate on Christmas carols, particularly popular with village boys and girls. The general opinion was that they should be kept up for New Year, that just as the Christians had made good use of pagan customs, the communists should do the same with Christian customs. Better not to lose folk tradition but to eradicate religion by education. Always education and not coercion is the key word. Easter, the most observed feast in Orthodox countries, is kept up with Easter eggs and the eating of a special Easter cake. The harvest festival is a popular occasion.

My own experience thoroughly confirmed the tolerant attitude shown in these many discussions. I was there at the invitation of a communist minister who knew my position. I was left entirely free by everyone concerned to choose my own translators who could play a big role in the view that I took. I chose them for their knowledge of English and their compatibility, not from selected candidates but through friends. It so happened that my companions on all my travels had no party connections. For obvious reasons I preferred it that way. I wished to preserve my objectivity and I might easily have been pushed in an opposite direction by a guide who was trying too hard. It might also have inhibited the many discussions I had with chance acquaintances. As I have already said, not one of these people unknown to me previously criticised the conception of the People's Republic but a few were very outspoken in their opinion of individuals, as free as I would be in discussing some official at home. This freedom lent weight to their opinions.

All that I have written naturally applies only to Bulgaria but, from a briefer and more restricted experience in the USSR and other communist countries, I always found, in privacy at any rate, a far greater frankness than anyone who had not been there would think possible, let alone the regular reader of *Time* magazine.

14. WHAT THE BULGARIAN READS

LITERATURE

Bulgaria as a 'new' country – her greatest writer Ivan Vazov only died in 1925 – naturally reads many translations, though she has a number of modern 'classics'* worthy of a world readership. Among them are the short-story writers Elin Pelin, who specialises in scenes of village life, and Yordan Yovkov, both contemporaries of the great Vazov, Dimiter Talev, whose *Iron Candlestick* gives a wonderful picture of the religious struggle in the 1830's and Dimiter Dimov, the author of a powerful novel, *Tobacco*. Poetry, however, predominates and in spite of a few excellent translations is not available to the foreigner. The Russian classics, almost universally known in the original and cheaper to buy in Bulgaria than in Russia itself, are so familiar as to be part of the pattern of thought. There is also the pride that Bulgaria played so large a part in spreading the Cyrillic alphabet.

Many English writers are known in translation. Shakespeare with *Hamlet* and *Macbeth* as favourites and also the sonnets which are frequently recited; *Robinson Crusoe, Gulliver's Travels*, some Scott, especially *Rob Roy* and *Ivanhoe*, Shelley, Byron's *Childe Harold* and the *Giaour*, most of Dickens, the Brontës, with *Jane Eyre* and *Wuthering Heights*, Oscar Wilde – *The Ideal Husband* ran

* See Bibliography, p. 184.

for three years in the national theatre – Shaw, in particular *Pygmalion*, *Candida* and *You Never Can Tell* – there is a Bernard Shaw postage stamp – and Galsworthy. *Treasure Island* and especially *Alice in Wonderland (Alissa v stranata na choudessata)*, with a new translation this year are great favourites and every child knows *Winnie the Pooh (Mecheto Pouch)* by heart. It also has been translated twice.

Successful translations have been a mixed bag with Bennett's *Old Wives' Tale*, Maugham's *The Razor's Edge* and *The Moon and Sixpence*, Conan Doyle's *The Hound of the Baskervilles*, much of Edgar Wallace, Graham Greene's *Our Man in Havana*, Kingsley Amis's *Lucky Jim* and John Braine's *Room at the Top* and *Life at the Top* and Sillitoe's *The Loneliness of The Long Distance Runner*. English humour is enormously appreciated. Among American writers, Mark Twain, Melville with *Moby Dick*, Cooper's *Last of the Mohicans*, Pearl Buck's books on China, Hemingway, Fitzgerald and Steinbeck and recently *To Kill a Mockingbird* and *The Catcher in the Rye*.

There is a great flow of contemporary fiction, some of it bad sentimental stuff like our own but also didactic and within the old-fashioned framework of a narrow 'socialist-realism'. It is the Party and the Komsomol who always come to the rescue. The subject of this type of romantic fiction the world over is good versus evil, with good triumphant. It all depends with whom one identifies good. I was delighted some years ago in reading a Russian novel, a very thrilling one, that was James Bond in reverse, minus the sadism and sex, with capitalists as the stick-at-nothing villains. Alter the names and it could have been published with success by a publishing house sponsored by the John Birch Society. I suspect that fortunately readers pay little attention to the political bias but read on for the story, though some of the hate and violence may influence the feeble minded. Recently there has been a change in the light fiction, it has become more human, less naïve and consequently more truly realistic; the party secretary is not now always heroic *ex officio*.

Bulgaria has its Maigret, or more nearly, its Sherlock Holmes, a delightful creation, Avakum Zachov by Andrei Gouliashki. He is

G

an archaeologist by profession with an interest in mathematics and, of course, a great psychologist. He is also very much a ladies' man. These books, two of which I have read in French, are splendidly written, sophisticated and with the characterisation and expertise that makes such books credible and enjoyable. Zachov helps the police in dealing with spies and traitors. The enemy is not mentioned by name and there is no incentive to hate. One of the books, *Midnight Adventure*, has been filmed, another is about to be translated into English, which will afford a painless way of taking a look at the other world.

The Bulgarians have always been a poetry conscious people and the poetry is on a much higher level than the prose, is constantly quoted, read and discussed. The poet has at all times been treated with exceptional respect. A standard is set by the literary magazine, *The Flame*, that publishes prose, poetry and criticism. *The Literary Front*, a weekly, also publishes original work and criticism. The criticism is naturally on party and literary lines which are made to merge. The supreme sin is 'art for arts sake', which may once have had some meaning but which has long been abandoned here. George Orwell, no friend to communism, in his *Essay on Dickens* wrote that all art is propaganda. The only question is, propaganda for what? To the communist neither science nor art can be unpolitical. It is either Marxist or it is not, there is no middle position. In revolution this is a source of strength, in stable times it can be a danger.

There is since Stalin's death a wind of change, not in the Marxist canon itself but in the greater tolerance with which it is stated and in the accent on spiritual values. That, properly understood, is a possible meeting point, as long as we do not see in it any weakening of Marxism. Liberalism in our sense of the word is not accepted. The radical is often to the left of the communist. We too have a load of materialism to shed before coming down to essentials.

I believe that Bulgaria has an important role to play in providing a meeting point and maintaining peaceful coexistence. She is small enough not to have vast political or military ambitions, she is the closest of all countries to Russia in sympathy yet indepen-

dent minded, she has always shown herself exceptionally tolerant, she has now become a meeting place for tourists from all
nations.

THE PRESS

The format of the newspapers follows closely that of Russia.
It is forbidding in the extreme both in typography and content
and might well take some leaves from the pages of *The Daily
Worker* without imperilling – I was about to write – its immortal
soul.

The whole conception of a newspaper is different from the west.
The *Daily Worker*, *l'Humanité* and especially the Italian *Unità*
seem sophisticated and even a trifle frivolous judged by eastern
standards. A communist newspaper must inspire and exhort and
to do this daily means a hoarse and strident voice, a paucity of
adjectives and an overwhelming number of statistics of the
'before and after' variety. If in our popular press it is only necessary
to read 50 per cent of a sentence to seize its meaning, 30 per cent
would be the amount there. I looked at the papers regularly. Here
is a representative day.

The leading paper is *Rabotnichesco Delo* (Workers' Deeds), the
organ of the Central Committee of the Communist Party and
therefore equivalent to the Russian *Pravda*. It consists of four
pages, six on Sunday.

The issue I have selected, a typical one, had a two-column
leading article in heavy type on ideological propaganda. 'This must
be made more persuasive. Lectures should be well informed, etc.,
etc.' All of it was dull and all completely obvious. I am not com-
plaining about the bias, I have taken it for granted and admitted
that while I cannot conform I hold it in very considerable respect.
The point that I am making is that at this stage of communist
development it is surely ineffective and will become increasingly
negative. I asked a group of people, party members among them,
if they had read this particular article. No one had. I would suggest
some consumer research among the under thirties.

There was news about Vietnam; this had been read with interest
and indignation. It was accompanied by a cartoon, American style

in reverse. The remainder of the front page was taken up with accounts of various functions, the opening of exhibitions, the unveiling of a monument, the award of Cyril and Methodius medals for active propaganda workers, who was there and what was said. There was a smudgy photograph of shock workers of a village in the south who had harvested fifteen hundred *dekars*, accompanying an article 'Agricultural tasks on time'.

The second page was devoted to internal news, mainly on new developments and industrial achievements. There was the rubric 'Deeds of Moral Beauty', with stories of how a Pioneer had saved another Pioneer from drowning and of the bravery and self-sacrifice of workers in a gas explosion. There were, from my point of view, two really interesting articles: a reportage on Levski's house in Karlovo to which a new exhibition hall had been added and one on life in the Rhodope Mountains. But there is no need to continue in detail page by page. More Vietnam, including a poem on a North Vietnam hero, Tran Van Dong, executed in Saigon. He was compared to Giordano Bruno. I was told that this was well written. News from the USSR and the communist parties abroad. There was one exceptional item, the story of a crime and a request from the police to trace the murderer of the cashier of the Central Council of the Bulgarian Union for Physical Culture and Sport who had been robbed of some thirteen thousand *leva*. This piece of negative news was obviously only printed for a positive reason, the appeal to the public for information. The sports coverage was excellent.

It is an extraordinary thing how very well informed people are and how quickly news that is not published gets around. It is partly the experience of reading the news behind the news, the news between the lines, an experience quickly acquired as we realised during the war when we read 'the situation is confused' and knew that it meant a defeat. Foreign broadcasts when listened to are used purely for the pop music which is often tape recorded, anything from *émigré* sources is so suspect as to defeat its own object and 'The Voice of America', when not jammed, is considered far too naïve.

A far more readable and better produced paper was the *People's*

Youth, published daily, except on Thursday when an eight page weekly, *Students' Tribune*, appears in its place. Apart from the news and pep articles, more attractively presented and with an excellent coverage of the arts, there were many features; a serial 'The Memoirs of a Bulgarian Spy in World War II', an imaginary crime to be solved, a competition for youth activity in amateur dancing, acting, music, library service, study of the heroic past, the aesthetic education of youth and so on. There were three first prizes of television sets, three second prizes of tape recorders and three third prizes of gramophones to be given to the organisation involved. That night's TV programme was 'An evening dedicated to Vazov', a Rumanian film and 'What to do on Sunday'. There was an article on the Nazis in West Germany, well documented and calmly written, and various items from the west, factual, usually derogatory and out of context. Sport was given much space.

There were also some advertisements of ready-made dresses for children and school notices. This paper was read not only by the young but by very many older people. It is a good sign that the paper of the younger generation has a livelier approach.

In communist countries there is no trace of militant feminism. Equality has long been admitted but this has not been distorted to imply that the sexes are identical and their interests the same, consequently women who do jobs that were once almost exclusively masculine, engineering for instance, retain all their femininity. The woman's magazine, often despised by our feminists, exists as in the west. It is a monthly, *Woman Today*, dealing in a practical way with mothercraft, cooking, careers and fashion. I was amused to see that it even had its 'sob-sister' page. 'I was a student in the top form when we married. I thought I would be happy but two weeks after our wedding my husband showed me his real character. He began beating me and didn't stop even when I was pregnant. He is a sordid man, he doesn't like laughter and gaiety. I am thinking seriously of divorce but I am pregnant again. I ask readers of this magazine who have suffered in this way to advise me. Would I be able to take care of the children on my own?'

This should prove reassuring to every westerner. Unfortunately

I did not read the replies but I am sure that they were full of stiff upper-lippery and sound common sense.

From my experience of the journalists themselves, and I met very many, I found them intelligent and very knowledgeable indeed about my particular subject. They had either prepared their homework with great care or knew it all before. The questions they asked were interesting to answer, devoid of gossip or trivialities, and always reported almost verbatim without the use of distorting headlines.

The newspapers obviously propound government policy and could not exist as an opposition. That does not mean that they are not sometimes critical, but never of aims, only of methods and achievements. For instance, during my time in Bulgaria, a series of open letters to officials were published by the excellent monthly *Youth*, magazine of the Central Committee of the Komsomol.

For the attention of the Minister of Trade:
Credit of up to fifteen hundred *lev* should be given to young families to furnish a home. There should be mobile canteens and deliveries from stores to help young mothers.

Goods for children, toys and clothing, should be greatly improved.

For the attention of the Committee for Work and Salaries:
Young mothers should be allowed to work at home, if possible. A special law must be passed for young mothers when they first return to work, allowing them to work for four hours instead of six hours.

For the attention of the Minister of Finance and Chairman of Trades Unions:
In order to increase building of kindergartens and nursery homes 50 per cent of what is gathered from self-taxation should be used for this purpose

The age for children's allowances should be increased to above sixteen. There should be radical increases in children's allowances for second, third and fourth children and the allowance for the first child done away with.

For the attention of the Minister of Public Health:
All big factories and cooperative farms should have special kitchens for babies and children.

For the attention of the Ministry of Defence:
Married soldiers should be granted longer leave.

For the attention of the Chairmen of People's Councils:
Special bureaux for child-care services should be organised so that all can find baby-sitters ... All cinemas, theatres and big shops should have children's rooms.

For the attention of the Central Council of the Sports Union:
There should be propaganda for more activities for young mothers with special care for their figures, in particular for the Turkish women in the Rhodope mountains.

And finally, the Central Committee of the Komsomol itself is urged to work for the introduction in schools of optional courses in Personal Hygiene and Sexual Knowledge, to be vigilant in the observance of the law that women should not do men's heavy work, to see that young married people are not kept apart by their work, to encourage an interest in fashion and to develop the minds and interests of young women especially in the villages.

I have not quoted these examples merely to show an important function of the Press, nor of that admirable institution the Komsomol, which could be so well adapted to our needs in the west, but also to underline a serious problem and the attention it is receiving.

HIGHBROW AND INTELLECTUAL: A DISCUSSION

The Foreign Language Press, a very well-run body to which I am greatly indebted, publishes a splendidly produced and well illustrated magazine *Bulgaria* in several languages. It often defeats its own object by overstating a good case and by trumpeting national achievements too loudly so that it arouses an attitude of resistance. The photographs, short stories and poems are far more revealing than the interviews with workers and intellectuals. I know only too well that the enthusiasm is real and that the interviews are genuine, but to the westerner they read as if they have been heavily edited. This is characteristic of a new and vital nation. I noticed it in the less sophisticated American and in the Australia of the 1930s, but it is also characteristic of communist propaganda in general. I have nothing against propaganda for an ideal so long as it is skilled. An example of propaganda that spoilt an excellent case by overreaching itself occurred in an exhilarating argument that I had with a very well informed and well disposed acquaintance who had read widely in English. We started talking about Sherlock Holmes and Maigret which we both enjoyed and Bulgaria's own detective, Avachum Zachov. He went on, 'Your agent 007, James Bond, appeals to the very worst instincts in people. He is both a sadist and a masochist, a coldblooded murderer and a voluptuary. His attitude to women is revolting. His great popularity is a sign of real degeneracy in the west. What makes it worse is the cult of these books among intellectuals.'

I agreed with him up to a point. 'This is unhealthy stuff. Personally I find it much more pornographic than *Fanny Hill*, for instance, especially when filmed, and I know very many people who would agree, but you overrate what you call this cult. What amuses the intellectual is the author's expertise in descriptions of meals, gambling and so on. It is not taken seriously, especially politically.'

'I disagree,' he replied, 'its predecessors *Bulldog Drummond* and Buchan's stuff are very thinly disguised fascism and generations have been brought up on them.'

'I have revelled in Buchan, I admit. He is a superb story-teller, but once again I must insist that I take it as very light escapist entertainment.'

'You may, but to me it is an example of the weary oversophistication that I deplore. To the millions of readers of this stuff it must convey a powerful message.'

'I doubt it, it is pure fantasy, as much a flight from reality as any fairy tale.'

'I agree about the fantasy and that is my whole point. It is in fantasies and fairy tales that people truly reveal themselves and this is an exceptionally ugly revelation.'

He had made a strong point, but then he continued,

'And, of course, this stuff is put out deliberately to foster hatred and to excuse the cruelty of napalm and so on and so forth.'*

And here in the use of the word *deliberately* he had completely misunderstood the position and weakened a strong case. I continued,

'James Bond, agent 007, is not the result of any policy, governmental or otherwise. Unlike the Beatles, Ian Fleming was not given any official recognition. His only motive was to write for hard cash, following Dr Johnson's famous dictum.'

He did not reply with the obvious, that to peddle such stuff for money could be said to be an unworthy motive in itself, neither did we start another argument on the pros and cons of censorship. He was simply not convinced that this was not all part of a deliberately fostered imperialist plot. We agreed to differ over a drink. It showed me the gulf that can exist between two people who agreed in fundamentals, a gulf caused by a faulty knowledge of the working of the western mind. No doubt we are equally ignorant of their way of thinking, especially their earnestness, the literal way in which they take things and their distrust of flippancy. The words 'intellectual' and 'intelligentsia' as opposed to 'highbrows' and 'eggheads' should give us a valuable clue. The highbrow can play with such toys as comic-strips, pop art, the Beatles and this same James Bond without abdicating his position. He does not say, 'I enjoy these things in my idle moments. They are fun.' He fits them into his system with an elaborate series of arguments. He cannot let himself be carried away by jazz without invoking Bach. He is not prepared to admit that a toy is a toy and leave it at that. The Slav intellectual has never gone in for such super-sophisticated

---

* Since this was written I was delighted to read in *The Times* that Bond is to be the villain in an Avakum Zachov novel, an admirable solution to the argument. 'Not a hair of James Bond's head will be touched', says Gouliashki, 'The conflict will be resolved in the aspect of humanism. English readers need not worry about their favourite. I am not going to make him out worse than Fleming did. They will meet on the Black Sea coast and the action will take them to Vienna, Greece and the Mediterranean. Of course Bond will fall in love with a Bulgarian girl – in his own way'.

We must wait a year or two for this treat. It will certainly be more realistic than the Lonsdale and Penkovsky 'memoirs'!

games. Communism has merely accentuated his essential serious-
ness. The Bulgarian intellectual is less intense than the Russian,
more of a belly-laugher, when he enjoys something outside his
serious interests he does not attempt to justify it. He is not apolo-
getic about belonging to the 'intelligentsia'. No one is proud of
being a lowbrow.

There is another essential difference that we must understand;
the difference between 'pop', which has a highly commercial
implication and *narodny*, of the people, part of the peasant heritage,
and therefore something to be cherished as an heirloom, a symbol
of identity.

The controversial question of socialist realism in art arises out
of this, and many of us have reacted against it instinctively.
Realism in itself is not a bad thing; Courbet was a realist. What is
bad is photographic naturalism and official idealisation. A true
artist, such as the Boyana master, will communicate in spite of the
most rigid canons. The notion that a bad painter will become a
good painter if he is allowed complete freedom is belied by history.
There may be sound moral reasons for allowing the artist complete
freedom, but that is another matter. 'Your western artists are not
free,' said a museum official, 'they are part of a great commercial
racket in which dealers and critics dictate to them what sells and
then a vast propaganda machinery is set into motion to protect the
investment. The ordinary man is ashamed to admit that he can
make neither head nor tail of the latest thing. Like women's
fashions there must be constant changes from *dada* to surrealism,
from tachisme, action painting to pop and op. We protect our
public from such assaults on taste and pocket.'

Here then is the other side of the picture. Perhaps after all this
is not a very good moment for painting in any part of the world.

15. THE BULGARIAN AT HOME

FAMILY LIFE

From what has gone before the reader will have been able to gain some impression of daily life in Bulgaria. The Bulgarian is essentially a home lover; frugal, temperate, dogged and exceedingly hard working. He can be argumentative and the peasant is something of a rough diamond, but of all the eastern Europeans he is the least excitable. He is intensely patriotic, loving his soil and proudly conscious of his heritage but no one is less of a xenophobe. Nowhere in my wanderings did I meet with a trace of suspicion or hostility. Every door was open and on more than one occasion did I meet with a 'why are you staying in a hotel when we could put you up?' His interest in education and the possibilities of self-improvement are boundless. He treats his children as individuals. They have plenty to say for themselves and are high spirited but courteous and well behaved.

Girls and boys go out together in groups but individual dating is very carefully vetted by parents, who beyond any shadow of doubt have the last word, neither was it questioned by any of the young people I met. At the seaside where life is very free and easy I never saw anything that would bring a blush to the cheeks of Dr Billy Graham.

An outing to the theatre or cinema is a valued treat. Perhaps the word treat is misleading, to the intellectual the theatre is almost a necessity and my friends went to theatre, opera or concert on an average of six times a month. Family picnics with parents and grandparents are a regular weekend event. People do not only enjoy things as spectators, they act and make music in schools and clubs, even in the heart of the country. There are admirable opportunities for learning an instrument in the library clubs (*chitalishte*), which were started under the Turkish yoke. Here children from five upwards can get excellent tuition in languages and music. There is a club in every city district and in many villages. The accordion is an extremely popular social accomplishment but also the violin and piano, so that music in the home is beginning to flourish. It is very much an echo of the pre-Freudian, pre-1914, middle-class life of England and America. Paradoxically, the revolution in family life that has taken place in the west has not touched this revolutionary republic.

We were frequently invited home by the children to meet the whole family and that often included uncles, aunts and cousins. It struck me particularly that on the occasions when the elders were obviously peasants and the next generation university graduates the old folk were always listened to with the greatest respect. No one appeared embarrassed by Uncle's long stories which must have been heard *ad nauseam*, on the contrary, the old boy would receive encouraging applause.

Mother cooked, sometimes the daughter would prepare a special dish and father discussed the wine, describing the particular vineyard with nostalgic detail. In the new flats the kitchens were modern and labour saving and there was generally a refrigerator.

There were far more books around than one would see in the average English home but pictures and ornaments were not conspicuous for their taste and more than one home had a vase of plastic flowers – in a land of flowers! Nearly everyone had a television set and a record player.

Sometimes we were invited to weekend bungalows, simple do-it-yourself structures in beautiful surroundings, with small well-kept gardens and a vine-covered portico for meals. Many who can afford such bungalows prefer to invest in a car so that they can camp in the many sites provided or travel to neighbouring countries. All such property belongs to the owner and can be willed to his children. Flats, bungalows and furniture can be bought through bank loans, repayable over a period of twenty years.

The family usually consists of one or two children. Birth control is not discussed though tacitly accepted; abortion is legal. Prenatal care is considerable. Most children are born in hospital and afterwards a nurse calls weekly for the first few months. Infant mortality, once the highest in Europe, is now one of the lowest in the world. Medicine is free and there are sixteen doctors* to every ten thousand inhabitants. Some doctors have private patients but private practice is not pensionable. The older members of the family are not only cherished, they have a very positive role to play and without them the family structure would collapse. *Baba* (Granny) is worth her weight in gold. This has always been the case, in the Balkans as in southern Europe, so that living together and pooling resources not only presents no hardship but preserves a traditional way of life.

There is always the problem of the ailing and incapacitated. There are homes to which they can be sent but it is considered a disgrace for any family to do so unless it is absolutely unavoidable.

I have already written of the adaptation of church festivals. There are public holidays on January the first, May the first and second, Labour Day, May the twenty-fourth, Cyril and Methodius Day of Culture, September the ninth and tenth, Liberation by the Russian army and November the seventh, the October revolution. There is a particularly charming unofficial holiday on March the

* In England three or four.

first when everyone wears a favour, *Martenitsa*, of red and white silk or cotton. This is given to friends or sent on a greetings card and signifies health and the beginning of a new life cycle. In the villages it is worn until you see the first stork or swallow and then, if it is buried under a stone, all your wishes will be fulfilled. The cat also is associated with spring and a black cat on a postcard is a form of greeting.

There is another unofficial day of celebration, March the eighth, International Women's Day. Children give flowers to their women teachers, women shock workers are awarded prizes and, of course, mother is remembered. 'All other days of the year,' said a friend, 'are father's days.'

It is difficult to estimate the cost of living and completely meaningless to do so by translating *leva* into pounds. I can only write from personal observation. Wherever I went, in town or country, I saw no evidence of poverty in the essentials of clothes, food, housing and mental and physical recreation. When invited to a meal the hospitality was lavish by any standard but, on the many occasions on which I dropped in for pot luck, the meal was simple but ample and of excellent quality; made up from such things as soup, eggs, bread and cheese, yoghourt, various kinds of sausage, salads, vegetables and always a variety of fruit in season.

Incomes are low and most people regard child allowances as inadequate but there is a considerable invisible income in free medicine and education, rest homes at a nominal sum, children's camping holidays, heavily subsidised canteen meals at places of work. Salaries and the price of living are carefully balanced. Food and housing appeared to me to be cheap, clothing expensive. Pensions are given at a comparatively early age. The individual might find it a struggle but the pooled resources of the family make living easier. The standard of living is certainly rising and I noted the difference in the year that I had been absent, especially in the more fashionable clothing of the women and the far better window displays in the big stores.

THE YOUNG MARRIED COUPLE

I have as a general rule foresworn statistics and this section may be skipped, though these are exceptionally revealing of attitudes and tendencies, of the standard of living and of the future. I have only dealt with the majority figures and there were the usual abstentions. It confirmed many of my own observations and did not surprise me, but as I only met some twenty families, mainly among the intelligentsia, my own unsupported picture would be unconvincing and incomplete.

The material for this wholly statistical but altogether human section comes from an investigation of 5037 young families made by the magazine *Youth* from a sample of 61·5 per cent manual workers, 13·4 per cent peasants, 25·1 per cent white-collar workers and intellectuals. It had greatly interested all the young people I knew.

The length of marriage of those asked: 3·8 per cent less than three months, 15·2 up to one year, 26·3 to three years, 19·4 to five years, 35·3 over five years; 87 per cent of the wives worked, 55·8 of the couples lunched in a canteen, 4 brought food to work, 0·5 lunched in a restaurant and the remainder at home; 44·7 per cent lived on their own, apart from their parents, 18·8 received some financial help from their parents, 29·8 helped their parents, 66·3 were able to save money, 25·7 were in debt after their wedding.

The average age of marriage for 80·5 per cent of the women was from eighteen to twenty-three years and of 55 per cent of the men from twenty-three to twenty-eight years; the average difference in age, five years. The majority had known one another from one month to two years and had met at work, school or university (35·6 per cent) or at the Komsomol (33·1). In 77·1 per cent of the cases under review it was the man who suggested marriage. The paper's comment is interesting, it finds the woman's percentage too low.

The household commodities enjoyed were: washing machines by 55·9 per cent, electric stoves 32·4, vacuum cleaners 17·1, refrigerators 9·3, TV sets 19·6.

To the question, have you a room together? only 0·6 per cent replied no, 16·3 had rooms allotted by the state in connection with their work, 35·5 had two rooms or more, 18·7 had invested in flats. This involved a down payment and twenty years in which to pay off the debt. The flat then belonged to them absolutely and could be given or left to the children. Their stated ambitions were for a flat, a TV set, a tape recorder, a car; in that order. For their holidays 35·3 per cent went to holiday resorts, 28·2 stayed at home, 3·6 went abroad. Leisure time was spent by 58·9 of men and women in reading and house work, 32·1 in listening to music, TV and further education. As many as 55 per cent did voluntary social work.

When asked how many children they wanted no one said none, 27·34 men and 28·1 women said one child, 54·5 men and 57·6 women said two, the remainder three or more. The small family is the rule in Bulgaria today due to economic conditions. This clearly worries the authorities, as one can see from the Komsomol magazine's suggestions.

Now for feelings and opinions.

Are your expectations of marriage fulfilled? 66·7 yes, 7 more than fulfilled, 21·2 disappointed.

Would you divorce? Never in any circumstances, 47·3 men, 58·2 women.

In fact the divorce rate has remained very low in villages. In 1962, 2,808 village divorces, 5,311 in cities; 10·1 per 10,000 of the population.* The main causes for quarrels, not necessarily leading to divorce, were disagreement about finance and household chores, the upbringing of children, housing, the influence of in-laws and moral questions, in that order. Cruelty was too rare to be listed.

When asked about pre-marital intercourse 42·2 of the men and 24·1 of the women found it acceptable for both parties so long as it was not promiscuous, of these 30 per cent added that there must be real love and 48 per cent that it should be a prelude to marriage.

Editorial comment seemed to think that women in general did not play a big enough role in life, though to the question, who is the boss at home? 28·5 replied men, 33·9 women. I should have said from observation that the man was the boss. 'The house is unhappy when the hen crows', says a popular proverb.

---

* This low divorce rate is remarkable for a country where divorce is comparatively easy. In all cases, especially where there are children, the courts try to bring about a reconciliation

16. RENVOI:

AN INTERVIEW ON A RAILWAY STATION PLATFORM

Q   Now that you have gathered all your material will you return to Bulgaria or is it a closed book?

ALH   I have every intention of returning. This is only a beginning. So far I have just learnt what to look for and where to look for it. In any case there are so many friends I want to meet again, so many interrupted discussions to be resumed.

Q   What made the greatest impression on you?

ALH   The spirit of Koprivshtitsa, that is something organic, Liliana Dimitrova, the girl herself and her heritage, the tremendous importance you attach to education and the fine products of that education, but, most of all, the vast implications of your tourist programme of three million by 1980. You are a compact country with a strong personality in close spiritual and physical contact with the USSR, a country whose vast and complex civilisation is enigmatic and frightening to so many. Now think of it, hundreds and thousands of people will, because of the sun and the amenities you have provided, visit a communist country for the first time. Instead of thinking, or rather not thinking, lazily in meaningless abstractions, 'they are all "reds", they will think in terms of friendly and cheerful individuals, of Bulgarians as neighbours, Dimiter, Donka and their kids. In your turn you will meet not reactionary capitalists but John, Mary and their kids.'

This is a simplification and slogans will not disappear overnight. At first there may be the qualification, 'they are nice in spite of being of such and such a colour'. Then may follow the thought, 'but what is it they actually believe and how do they put their beliefs into practice?' And this is the beginning of wisdom.

We shall probably agree to differ in our beliefs but to realise that their sincere practice leaves us a vast common territory. This would be the basis for something more than coexistence, a limbo as negative and arid as the sound of the word itself. After all, we did more than coexist at the singing, chamber music and ballet festivals in which we collaborated.

Q   And is there a reverse to the medal?

ALH Yes. You may go too far in providing the tourist with what he gets at home and what you think he wants. In this way you will not only give a distorted view of yourselves but you may actually come to believe in it.

There is nothing sadder than the phrase, 'you should have known such and such a place before the tourists spoilt it'. In fact the tourist does not spoil places without a great deal of help and encouragement from the people on the spot. Sunny Beach cannot be Monte Carlo but, alas, neither can Monte Carlo today.

Q   Do you yet know what type of book you will write?

ALH My title *Heroes and Roses* is the programme. I will not deal with very many of the things that are foremost in people's thoughts here; industrialisation, agriculture and economics. I am ignorant of those subjects and they have already been covered in year books and reports. These achievements are obvious. I am concerned with the type of people who made them possible, something that no set of statistics can reveal.

Q   One final question; will the book be of interest to Bulgarians?

ALH   From the point of view of information definitely not; you know it all, the information came from you. The interest could be in seeing what a well-wisher has considered important. You may disagree with much that I have written and that in itself could be interesting. You may think I have had insufficient time in which to get to know you. That is possible. This is a set of impressions that might have been dulled by a very long stay. To me, however, those impressions have been so vivid that the word 'Bulgaria' will always mean more friendship.

I am reconciled to the fact that some unthinking ones in both our countries may feel that I am a *red* or a *fascist*. I shall not lose any sleep over that.

Our friends throng the platform with flowers, wine, fruit and souvenirs – 'Good-bye until next year.'

BIBLIOGRAPHY

Some easily available books on Bulgaria in English and French.

HISTORICAL

Mercia Macdermott, *A History of Bulgaria, 1393-1885*, Allen & Unwin 1962

D. Kossev, H. Hristov, D. Angelov, *A Short History of Bulgaria*, Foreign Languages Press, Sofia 1963

POLITICAL, ECONOMIC AND SOCIAL

Stella Blagoeva, *Georgi Dimitrov*, Foreign Languages Press, Sofia 1961

The Leipzig Fire Trial – speeches, letters, documents, Foreign Languages Press

Spass Roussinov, *Bulgaria. Land Economy Culture*, Foreign Language Press, Sofia 1965

Nicolas Filtchev, *l'Intelligentsia en Bulgarie*, Editions en langues étrangères, Sofia 1961 (and in English).

Institute of Economics, *Social and Economic Development of Bulgaria, 1944–1964*, Foreign Languages Press, Sofia 1964

R. Polyakova and A. Dimov, *How the Bulgarian worker lives*, Foreign Languages Press, Sofia 1964

Bocho Iliev, *Management, Organisation and Labour Payment in Cooperative Farms*, Foreign Languages Press, Sofia 1963

Pensions in the People's Republic of Bulgaria, Foreign Languages Press, Sofia 1962

Professor Georgi Golubov M.D., *People's Health in The People's Republic of Bulgaria,* Foreign Languages Press, Sofia 1962

Nikolai Zagorski, *Peasant Life in Bulgaria,* Foreign Languages Press, Sofia 1964

Georgi S. Kolimachkov, *Education in Bulgaria,* Foreign Languages Press, Sofia n.d.

THE ARTS

Athanas Bojkov, *Les Arts Plastiques en Bulgarie,* Editions en langues étrangères, Sofia 1964

Dimiter P. Dimitrov, *Bulgaria land of Ancient Civilisations,* Foreign Languages Press, Sofia 1961

La Culture Médiévale Bulgare, Editions en langues étrangères, Sofia 1964

Boris Kolev and Ilia Boudinov, *Koprivshtitsa,* Bulgarski Houdozhnik Publishing House, Sofia 1957

Cyril Tsonev, *Frescoes in Boyana Church,* Bulgarski Houdozhnik Publishing House, Sofia n.d.

Milko Bichev, *Architecture in Bulgaria,* Foreign Languages Press, Sofia 1961

Konstantin Holachev and Serafim Severnyak, *Plovdiv,* Foreign Languages Press, Sofia 1965

Svetline Bossilkov, *Turnovo, La Ville et son art,* Editions Balgarski Houdozhnik, Sofia 1960

L'Opera en Bulgarie, Editions en langues étrangères, Sofia 1962

L. Shaoulov, *The Bulgarian Theatre*, Foreign Languages Press, n.d.

Woodcarving in Bulgaria, Foreign Languages Press, Sofia 1962

Galerie Nationale de Sofia, Publication rédigée par des collaborateurs près de la galerie Nationale, Sofia 1960

GUIDE AND TRAVEL BOOKS
Harold Rose, *Your Guide to Bulgaria*, Alvin Redman, London 1964

Mathieu Corman, *Drougar*. Vie intime d'une république populaire, Tribor, Bruxelles n.d.

Edouard Calic, *Life in Bulgaria*, Foreign Languages Press, Sofia 1964

Stowers Johnson, *Gay Bulgaria*, Robert Hale, 1964

Bulgaria Through the Eyes of Foreigners, Foreign Languages Press, Sofia 1959

MAGAZINES PUBLISHED IN ENGLISH
Bulgaria, Foreign Languages Press (monthly)
Resorts, Balkan Printing House (bimonthly)

FICTION
Ivan Vazov (translated by Marguerite Alexieva and Theodora Atanassova), *Under the Yoke*, Foreign Languages Press, Sofia 1960

Ivan Vazov (translated by Roger Bernard), *Sans Feu ni Lieu*, Editions en langues étrangères, Sofia 1963

Dimiter Dimov (translated by Georges Assen Dzvigov), *Tabac*, Editions en langues étrangères, n.d.

Dimiter Talev (translated by Marguerite Alexieva), *The Iron Candlestick*, Foreign Languages Press, Sofia 1964

Elin Pelin (translated by Marguerite Alexieva), *Short Stories*, Foreign Languages Press, Sofia 1965

In the Fields – Bulgarian Short Stories, Narodna Kultura, Sofia 1957
Eline Peline (translated by Roger Bernard), *Sous la treille du Monastère*, Editions en langues étrangères, Sofia 1963

Yordan Yovkov (translated by Roger Bernard), *Légendes de la Stara Planina*, Editions en langues étrangères, Sofia 1963

Pavel Veginov (translated by S. Goranova and T. Chepkov), *Les Traces demeurent*, Editions en langues étrangères, Sofia 1964

Andrei Gouliashki, *Mission à Momtchilovo*, 1962.

La Belle du bois dormant, 1964, Les Editeurs Français Réunis, Paris

POETRY
Geo Milev (translated by Peter Tempest), *September*, Foreign Languages Press, Sofia 1961

SOME EARLY BOOKS
G. Muir Mackenzie and A. P. Irby, *Travels in the Slavonic Provinces of Turkey in Europe*, Bell and Daldy, 1867

Lady Grogan, *The Life of J. D. Bouchier*, Hurst and Blackett 1926

A. de Lamartine, Souvenirs, Impressions, Pensées et Paysages pendant un *Voyage en Orient* 1832–1833, Vol. II, 1887

INDEX